AMERICA, DEMOCRACY

&You

Where have all the citizens gone?

AMERICA, DEMOCRACY & *You*

Where have all the citizens gone?

Ronald R. Fraser, Ph.D.

CHESHIRE & COMPANY
VIEWPOINTS PUBLISHING, INC.

WEST FALLS, NEW YORK

Published by The Cheshire & Company Viewpoints Publishing, Inc.

7744 Center Road, West Falls, NY 14170

Cheshire_Publishing@roadrunner.com

(716) 941-5986

www.smalltowncivics.com

Grateful acknowledgment is made to:

The American Political Science Association for permission to use, in Chapter 1, segments from *American Democracy in an Age of Rising Inequality*, (2004);

UNIVERSAL UCLICK for permission to reprint, from the Washington Post, three Tom Toles cartoons;

The University of California at Berkeley, Department of Geography, for permission to use, in Table 4, material from The Living New Deal website, and

W.W. Norton & Company, Inc., for permission to quote in Chapter 4 from Edmund S. Morgan's, *Inventing the People: The Rise of Popular Sovereignty in England and America*, (1988).

Cover/Interior Design ©2015 Leslie Taylor, buffalocreativegroup.com

Printed in the United States of America

First Edition: October 2015

ISBN: 978-0-578-17047-3

Library of Congress Control Number: 2015917095

For

PJ, Annie Gail, Dylan Joe and a cat named Felix

Contents

Foreword

Are you disaffected from politics? Do you feel politically powerless? Are you angry when you read the headlines? There is a wide range of citizen reactions to politics, from confusion, to disgust, to protest. The current climate alternates between "it's all their fault," to "there's nothing I can do," to "I am angry."

Fraser's book gives you the concepts and tools to help you analyze your reactions to our political system. What were you taught in school? Are "they"—the politicians and controlling interests—the reason you are not involved in public affairs?

Many who subscribe to the commonly affirmed statement that in a democracy the "people rule," will be surprised by Fraser's insistence that popular rule is basically a myth. He grounds this thesis in a historical review of the concept of "popular sovereignty." He compares the views of popular rule from the period of framing the Constitution, Andrew Jackson's presidency, the New Deal period, the early emphasis on rights rather than responsibilities. The comparison alerts us to the lack of a general consensus about public sovereignty and asks what are the uses and dangers of political myths? Do they guide our behavior? Do they blind us to reality? Do they lead to disillusionment?

Just as the view of "the people" has changed over time, the role and professionalization of government has changed as well. The economic development of society increased the role of organized interests while the citizen became primarily a consumer. There has also been a revival of the Founding Fathers' belief that the individual is mainly self-interested and not naturally inclined to focus on the common good. As a result the citizen is anything but sovereign. All of these changes are reflected in the myths that the public holds and leads to doubts about whether civic participation is useful or worth the trouble.

It is, however, still all too natural to subscribe to the myth of citizen rule given the view of civic and political participation taught through high school textbooks. These books and courses give a limited view of participation, play down the realities of the political process and do little to promote civic participatory skills.

The constant theme of this book is that there is a yawning gap between the realities of the political process and the persistence of the myth that the people rule and the need for you to reconcile the realities you experience and myths you believe in.

Fraser gives his readers the analytic tools to analyze their styles of democratic citizenship and invites us to examine what we feel about the public's role and how we assess the realities of political life. While many works focus on the power of organized interests and elites, Fraser insists we, the citizenry, need to reflect on our role. To assist us, he suggests that we consider several types of participation. Do we feel comfortable with the civic role we have chosen for ourselves? Now that we can "name" our approach, are there parts of it we would like to change or develop?

Underneath everything he writes is the urgency of his belief that our democracy will not get better until there is greater involvement by citizens, that we will be motivated to take a hard look at our civic participation and decide whether we are content with it. Hopefully our analysis will awaken us to new possibilities and efforts.

Louise G. White
Professor Emeritus, George Mason University, Fairfax, Virginia

Preface

Why are so many Americans living in the world's most celebrated self-rule democracy overwhelmed with a serious case of political powerlessness? Something just does not add up. Listen to what Americans are telling the pollsters.

* * * * *

A 2004 opinion poll reported that, "Many Americans feel that they have lost influence over their own government and are looking for ways to regain control." More than 56% of those surveyed said lobbyists and 68% said large corporations and big campaign contributors have a great deal of influence over decisions in Washington. Only 20% of American citizens think the general public has a great deal of influence in Washington. (Hart, 2004)

And, in a 2011 poll, seven out of ten Americans—or, about 165 million American adults—claimed, "Elected officials don't care what people like me think," and "Elected officials quickly lose touch with voters back home." (Kohut, and others, 2011)

* * * * *

If you belong to this super majority, if you feel you have been abandoned by the American democracy, this book is written for you. While your feeling of powerlessness is real it's time you get a grip on why you feel the way you do and, most importantly, to do something about it. You don't need a Ph.D. to read this book. It is written for everyone, including my sister and members of her gardening club.

You can blame the top 1% ers, the Wall Street gamblers, and the home loan bankers. They are guilty as charged. But Pogo was right: "We have met the enemy and he is us." That's right. We citizens, you, me and millions of others, it turns out are a big part of the problem.

Elections are mainly an illusion of power, not the real thing. Until citizens, millions of us, begin acting like the owners of the American democracy, until we get involved between elections— when our elected representatives, out of public view, decide who gets what—we can continue to belly ache to pollsters and nothing will change. Real political power—political responsiveness— takes place between elections when big campaign financiers and swarms of lobbyists hired by special interest groups, not citizens, rule the policy making process.

Today we hear a lot more talk about economic inequality than we do about political inequality yet the two go hand in hand. Political power has a way of attaching itself to those people holding the economic power. As long as millions of American remain politically AWOL, putting their faith in political myths, not active citizenship, political elites and self-serving interest groups will continue to control, for their own benefit, both the political and the economic levers of power in America.

Over the last 200 years, as our political institutions have matured, public officials have learned to conduct the public's business with little or no meaningful citizen involvement in the governing process. In America's self-rule form of government you either get involved or someone else will take your place.

Think about it. What might happen if millions of sidelined citizens, now on the outside looking in, were to become politically active not just on election day but between elections as well? When citizens stay involved in the ongoing governing process, the corporate lobbyists will no longer determine who gets what. Political responsiveness will shift back to where it belongs, with the citizens.

Long ago, after political reality dashed too many of my own initial beliefs in the American system of government, I wanted to find out if democracy really exists in America. What follows is, in large part, an intellectual travel log of my own struggle to answer that question. I hope you find it a useful guide as you seek answers to your own questions concerning the American democracy and your place in it.

Who knows, this book just might become the roadmap you and millions of other out-of-the-loop citizens will use to put the American democracy back on track. Then again, it might confirm your worst fears, that a citizen-based democracy is doomed and, if it ever really existed, it is now an idea whose time has come, and gone. Either way, you win. Either way, the ideas in the following pages will most assuredly make you a wiser— whether energized or disengaged—citizen.

Ronald R. Fraser
August 2015

America, Democracy & You

Introduction

Sooner or later, most Americans discover that political reality and political promises don't match up. Once faced with reality, each of us must resolve this question: Does a self-rule democracy really exist in America; or is it a myth, existing mainly in the minds of its citizens?

To resolve this question Americans, one by one, pass through a three-part civic cycle:

1.) An initial acceptance of a fictionalized democracy received in school is followed by;

2.) A period of doubt which, in turn, is followed by;

3.) The adoption of a personal definition of American democracy based on one's first-hand experience of political reality.

While some citizens never consciously compare their schoolbook version of democracy with the real thing, it is clear to me that most Americans do, at some level of conscientiousness, progress through this three-part process. Some do it quickly, effortlessly. Others take their time and struggle to reconcile the two views of democracy.

Chapter Previews

Chapter One: Is a brief history of the role of citizens in the American democracy. This historical background will help the reader appreciate what it means to be a citizen today.

Chapter Two: Takes us inside American classrooms—citizen boot camps—where we'll look at how young citizens-to-be are being indoctrinated with a citizen-centered vision of democracy; a view based more on historic and political myths than everyday political reality.

Chapter Three: Here we'll take a look at what happens when schoolbook democracy collides with real-life democracy, as school kids mature into young adults and gain their own first-hand experience of the political world around them. Once aware that they are not the central feature of today's American democracy, most citizens want to blame someone or something for their loss. Some blame the rigged political system while others blame their own short comings.

    The writers cited in this chapter have produced a long list of excuses used by citizens to justify their failure to become politically involved. These excuses, smoke screens in my book, hide the root cause for the breakdown of self-rule democracy in America—an epidemic of inactive citizens.

Chapter Four: Largely hidden from sight, I will argue, political and historical myths—not a rigged political system—are the culprits. Myths tell Americans that they are the ultimate political power in our system of government and they buy it, even after the myths are shown, based on personal experience, to be false.

    Are the myths then discarded? No way. To retain their cherished belief that they are, in fact, the cornerstone of our democracy, Americans by the millions do a weird thing—they willingly suspended their disbelief and pretend the myths are true and that their self-rule government works as advertised.

    Your reaction, at first, might be to ask, "What in the world do myths have to do with American democracy?" But stick with it. Myths are a kind of super glue holding the American system together. The problem is this. While political myths are an essential part of the American democracy, they also give us permission to put our self-rule democracy on autopilot, they tell us that our participation in the governmental process is optional.

When citizens remove themselves from the civic arena, creating a political vacuum, into that vacuum rush self-serving interest groups seeking government favors. And, as the ability of interest groups to manipulate the government process goes up, the political power of citizens goes down. This is, I contend, the root cause of your feeling of political powerlessness.

Take your time with this chapter. Since you may not have given political myths a lot of attention in the past, now is a good time to consider how they work, how they form and shore up your beliefs in the American self-rule system of government.

Chapter Five: This is where you may reassess, and perhaps revise, your own personal civic role. You might find that you are content to remain a Civic Dropout. Or you might be challenged to become a Self-rule Idealist, or something in between. Either way, you will have gained a much better understanding of what it means to be an American citizen and, hopefully, a more comfortable personal view of your place in our democracy.

The goal is not to find a civic role that is "correct," but to discover the civic role that best fits your own experience-based definition of democracy and your place in it, or out of it, as the case may be.

Chapter Six: Where to from here?

* * * * *

CHAPTER ONE

Self-Rule Democracy: Citizens Optional?

"Legitimization of political power in a constitutional democracy is achieved by dividing and subdividing the power once held by a unitary sovereign monarch, until all citizens have come to share in it. Consequently, all share responsibility for the manner in which the power of the one-time sovereign is wielded...And the problem of the citizen's responsibility for government has become at least as important as that of the justification of his obedience to government."

(Spiro 1969, 8)

* * * * *

Tracing citizen participation from the nation's beginning will provide an historical context for the following chapters. This historical survey describes how, since July 4th 1776, the status of citizens in the governmental process has plummeted from the ultimate source of political power in 1776 to a feeling of political powerlessness today.

Building on this historical baseline, the following chapters will show that what it means to be an American citizen has long been, and still is, a moving target. Like all preceding generations, today's citizens are free to carve out a place for themselves in their democracy—or not.

The Declaration of Independence

"We hold these truths to be self-evident, that all men are created equal, that they are endowed by their Creator with certain unalienable Rights, that among these are Life, Liberty and the pursuit of Happiness—That to secure these rights, Governments are instituted among Men, deriving their just powers from the consent of the governed—That whenever any Form of Government becomes destructive of these ends, it is the Right of the People to alter or to abolish it..." (Declaration of Independence, July 4, 1776)

There it is, in black and white. Governments are not the source of fundamental political freedoms and rights. These freedoms and rights existed prior to the formation of the United States of America. Governments are formed not to give, but to protect these freedoms and natural rights and, to remain legitimate, governments must continue to receive the consent of the people they govern.

These principles existed long before 1776 and, shortly after the 13 English colonies declared themselves 13 sovereign American states, state constitutions followed suit and also placed governments' supreme political powers not in public institutions but in their citizens. Powerful stuff for sure and just what was needed to fire up a rebellion against England. The sovereign American people could not only create governments, they could abolish them as well.

But the shelf life of this power-to-the-people period was short. With revolt fever high in 1776, little thought was given to how this boundless authority in the hands of the people would be converted into practical, governing institutions in 1787.

Winning independence was one thing. Building a new American government was quite another.

The Constitution

Instead of drawing citizens into the governmental process, the original American Constitution requires only that you and I sit on juries when called, elect members of the House of Representatives and pay our taxes. Additional civic duties were left to be defined by future generations. And that is exactly what has happened.

In the 11years separating the Declaration of Independence and the drafting of the Constitution in Philadelphia, the once celebrated sovereign people lost much of its glitter. In 1776 most Americans were united by a single goal: gaining political independence from England. Eleven years later, in the summer of 1787, the goal was no longer winning independence but putting together a workable national government. Cooler heads looked for ways to control, not empower, the American people.

As the nation rapidly evolved socially and economically in the 1800s from a rural land to an urbanizing, industrializing nation, and as more and more citizens gained the right, citizen participation in the governing process skyrocketed only to later erode once again.

A Few Good Citizens Will Do (1789 to 1820s)

James Madison, a key architect of the Constitution, did not design the American government to change the nature of man. He first sized up the human condition and only then designed a form of government that took into account man's flawed character. Men, by nature, possess a limitless desire to compete for and acquire property and to use government powers—and even violence—to gain an economic advantage over others.

Madison was not about to repeat the failures of earlier Greek and Italian republics in which citizens took an active, direct role in the governing process. Lacking a homogenous citizen base, where all citizens shared similar private and public interests, these early republics eventually degenerated into economic class conflicts between the haves and the have-nots, anarchy or tyranny.

Since there was no way to prevent economic conflict among groups of citizens within a nation, Madison's government design was meant to purposefully accommodate class and interest group conflicts, not to eliminate them. Unlike the earlier republics that sought to replace economic class conflicts within the population with a common, civic spirit, Madison's governmental structure sought to control economic conflicts within the population and among organized interest groups by pitting groups against one another, thereby limiting the power of any one group to dominate the others and dictate public policies.

In addition, Madison wanted a system of government that would protect the economically well-off from the have-nots. Since the poor would always outnumber the rich in a republic, there was the danger that the less well-off masses could use the political process to redistribute wealth from the few wealthy to the many poorer citizens. Tyranny of the majority—the many have-nots using government to raid the property of the few haves—was to be prevented. Tyranny of the minority—a few wealthy citizens forming a plutocracy—was also to be avoided. How was this to be achieved?

First, geographically, the new American republic would be far larger than the earlier small European city state republics and would encompass many dispersed and economically diverse interest groups. Due to the enormous physical size of the American republic, self-serving groups would find it difficult to assemble and directly control the governmental process.

Since history showed that popular, participatory—also called direct—democracy was a breeding ground for violent group conflict, Madison also sought to remove citizens from having a direct role in the operation of the new nation. While the people might, in theory, possess the ultimate political power, their role was limited to electing honest men possessing civic virtue—that is to say, men who would put national wellbeing ahead of their own selfish and special interests—to represent them in the House of Representatives. Upon casting their ballots, citizens were expected to head for the political exit and wait for the next election to roll around.

Political stability was to be achieved by separating the politically sovereign people and their authority to establish governments from the delegated authority given to elected officials to actually govern, to run the day-to-day operation of the government. Too much direct government participation by the people would, reasoned Madison, only lead to conflict and instability, not popular control.

Finally, while economic class conflicts would continue, Madison counted on his famous checks and balances among the branches of government and on the virtuous elected representatives possessing a broad, national perspective to serve as a buffer between, and the means to control, economic class conflicts.

That, in a nutshell, is Madison's grand design.

* * * * *

"We the People of the United States ....do ordain and establish this Constitution for the United State of America." That first paragraph in the Constitution reaffirms that, as a political body, the American people alone possessed the power to form the new national government. But practical-minded men trying to design a functional government needed to balance the grand political philosophy promised in the Declaration of Independence with the not so grand nature of man. Taking no chances, Constitutional barriers were put in place to limit the peoples' participation in their government.

On Election Day, the people would only elect members to the House of Representatives. State legislatures, not the people, would select members to the U.S. Senate. And, to provide still another check in case the people wrongheadedly elected less than virtuous men to the House, the president would be selected by yet another independent body: an electoral college made up of appointed delegates from each state.

Madison did, however, use the concept of a single, collective, sovereign American people to ensure the new national government's absolute political independence from the states. While each American was already a citizen of his or her state, the new national Constitution created a second category of citizenship—a national citizenship. All existing state citizens thereby became separate citizens of the United States. This singular body of sovereign people—collectively all Americans—provided both the needed legitimacy for the new Constitution and authority to members of the U.S. Congress to regulate national affairs, issue currency, impose taxes, etc., independently from the 13 state governments.

Opposition to the Constitution

Not everyone rallied around the new Constitution. For one thing, it differed significantly from the existing state constitutions. State legislators, elected to one-year terms, gave voters a ready mechanism for holding elected officials accountable. In the new Constitution, where members of the House of Representatives were to be elected to two-year terms and the senators serving six-year terms, citizens would lose much of their ability to hold elected officials accountable. Opponents considered six-year senate terms as simply a way to establish an aristocratic body by another name and prompted Samuel Adams' famous warning that, "Where annual elections end, tyranny begins." (White 1939, 563)

Because states were geographically smaller, state citizens were physically closer to their state capitals. In addition, due to their physical proximity to their elected officials, state citizens were far more likely to become acquainted with the character and qualifications of candidates for state offices. These advantages would be lost in the much larger national government.

Furthermore, if citizens in the geographically smaller states were more likely to develop the necessary civic skills needed to perform their citizen duties and make self-rule work at the state level, opponents claimed that under the proposed federal Constitution, good citizenship would surely wither and die in the more populous and geographically much larger United States.

To calm widespread fears that the proposed Constitution gave too much power to the central government, state ratification conventions demanded that a Bill of Rights be added to protect the sovereign people from their own government. Ten amendments were added to the Constitution in 1791. But the unalienable right of the people to abolish abusive governments—a natural right declared in the Declaration of Independence—is nowhere to be found in either the original Constitution or amendments to the Constitution. (Today, more than a few Americans occasionally might, in fact, wish they had the power to abolish the government in Washington).

Civic Virtue

Republican governments had been around long before the American republic got its start in the late 1780s. Earlier republics required that legitimate governments must rule with the consent of the governed and must involve citizens of virtue in the governing process.

This relationship between the rulers and the people not only served as a hedge against corruption and tyranny but, more fundamentally, it underscored the need in a republic that private citizens must not be isolated from what takes place in the public arena, that their participation was an essential part of the governing process. In classical republicanism, good citizens do not put their own private well-being above the collective, public good.

The founders, however, openly worried that if the people— citizens and their elected representatives alike—lacked the desire and ability to place public, community-wide interests above their own self-interests, the American experiment might fail.

Madison, in Federalist Paper 51, published in the New York Packet on February 8, 1788, did not hide his concerns: "A dependence on the people is, no doubt, the primary control on the government; but experience has taught mankind the necessity of auxiliary precautions. In framing a government which is administered by men over men, the great difficulty lies in this: you must first enable the government to control the governed; and in the next place oblige it to control itself." (Hamilton, Madison and Jay 1911, 264)

Then, in Federalist Paper 55, published in the New York Packet seven days later, he explained why his American brand of republicanism relied more on institutional checks and balances, not virtue among the citizens to control the actions of men. He wrote: "As there is a degree of depravity in mankind which requires a certain degree of circumspection and distrust, so there are other qualities in human nature which justify a certain portion of esteem and confidence. Republican government presupposes the existence of these qualities in a higher degree than any other form. Were the pictures which have been drawn by the political jealousy of some [those in opposition to the proposed constitution] among us faithful likenesses of the human character, the inference would be, that there is not sufficient virtue among men for self-government; and that nothing less than the chains of despotism can restrain them from destroying and devouring one another." (Hamilton, Madison and Jay 1911, 286)

John Adams, an old-fashioned aristocrat, probably spoke for many others when, in 1788, he bluntly expressed his doubts about whether common men could rule themselves, when he wrote, "The proposition that [the people] are the best keeper of their liberties is not true. They are the worst conceivable, they are no keepers at all. They can neither act, judge, think or will." (Delli Carpini, and Keeter 1996, 35)

American-style Republicanism

The American Constitution also drew upon classical liberal ideas popularized by John Locke, Jean-Jacques Rousseau and John Stuart Mill, including the idea that individuals possessed certain natural rights which governments were bound to recognize and protect.

Unlike classical republicanism, with its emphasis on the public responsibilities of individual citizens to their community, the U.S. Constitution set in motion a rights-based form of republicanism. Self-centered citizenship was stressed above civic participation and community-wide responsibilities. The new Constitution marked an historic shift from classical republicanism to an American republicanism that clearly undervalued the role and status of citizen participation in the governing process.

And to emphasize the reach of the American republican experiment, the myth of the New American Character was born. Unlike rigid European societies, the new American enjoyed an equality where the self-made man could prosper socially and economically.

The Constitution also recognized a new kind of citizen, a new kind of political man. Obedience to kings and church authorities, a common practice in Europe, was rejected. The age of reason had arrived. Individuals, by nature, so the new thinking went, inherently possessed the necessary reasoning capabilities and free will to take responsibility for their own political fate by giving their consent to be governed, thereby spreading political responsibility to the people.

Once the idea that citizens were capable of governing themselves and able to accept responsibility for their own political well-being was accepted, it was then feasible to create gigantic representative governments in the name of its sovereign citizens.

Many Common Men Will Do (1820s to 1880s)

By the early 1800s America was known around the world as a new nation built on individual liberty. Later in the 1800s, social, religious, temperance, educational, health and women's rights movements put the idea of individual freedom into widespread practice, creating an era of both optimism and instability. As the nation grew politically, economically and geographically, a more upbeat view of human nature took root, replacing the preceding, elitist view that the masses could not be trusted to make sound political decisions. The common man is now thought to be inherently good, maybe even potentially perfectible.

In 1816, in a letter to Joseph Cabell, Thomas Jefferson seems to have anticipated the coming Jacksonian reforms. He wrote: "The way to have good and safe government, is not to trust it all to one, but to divide it among many…Where every man…feels that he is a participator in the government of affairs, not merely at an election one day in the year, but every day; when there shall not be a man in the State who will not be a member of some one of its councils, great or small, he will let the heart be torn out of his body sooner than his power be wrested from him by a Caesar or a Bonaparte." (Lipscomb and Bergh, 2000)

With Andrew Jackson's election to the White House in 1828, American politics took a radical, anti-aristocratic turn. A second uniquely American political experiment got underway that would morph the original republic into a popular democracy and, in the process, affirm individualism, equality and popular sovereignty as American ideals.

Jacksonian democracy, settlements in the western lands and wide ranging reform movements—all expressions of the populist wave sweeping across the nation in the 1800s—drew Americans into the public arena in ever larger numbers. Sometimes called

America's "Golden Age," between the 1840s and 1890s, the turn-out of the voting age population in presidential elections topped 80% in 1840, 1860 and 1876. In every presidential election between 1856 and 1896, voter participation exceeded 70%.

In modern day elections turnout rates have ranged between 58.2% in 2008 and 49% in 1996. (Univ. of California at Santa Barbara, The American Presidency Project)

What it meant to be an American also took shape during this period. More so than Europeans, Americans considered themselves individuals in a land of limited government; they distrusted strong, central governments and tended to trust the judgment of the common man over social and economic elites. Belief in the so-called American Creed—anti-strong central governments, individualism, egalitarianism and populism—not one's place of birth, defines who is an American.

Self-rule Comes of Age

America's self-rule experiment was finally taking off. Indentured servitude laws were disappearing, property ownership was becoming more common and, in western settlements, many more citizens became active, often out of necessity, in civic activities.

President Andrew Jackson detested the national government long dominated by its founding aristocrats. By the late 1820s, the nation's founders were rapidly passing into history. The only remaining signer of the Declaration of Independence, Charles Carroll of Maryland, died in 1832. Of the 39 signers of the Constitution, all had passed on except for William Few, from Georgia, who died in 1828, and the Virginian, James Madison, who lived until 1836.

Jackson's arrival in the White House opened the door wide for the involvement of citizens in public affairs. He championed frequent rotation of public office holders. The belief that ordinary citizens were fully able to fill public offices made some sense, since the services offered by public bureaus in those days were few and simple.

Election campaigns, a mixture of mass entertainment and politics, included political rallies, parades with marching bands and rousing campaign speeches. Courted by rival political parties, voters were rounded up, delivered to polling places, instructed on for whom to cast their ballot and, afterwards, re-warded with a token payment or a stiff drink. But once in power, political parties did little to push hard for social change, to en-franchise women or to undermine Jim Crow laws disenfranchis-ing southern blacks.

What victorious political parties did do, however, was fill government agencies with citizens lacking any qualifications for the job other than their loyalty to their elected political bosses. The growing need for more complex professional public services during the later 1800s, as the nation urbanized and industrial-ized, was largely ignored.

* * * * *

Curiosity about America and life in the New World prompted a Frenchman, Alexis de Tocqueville, to take a close look at the American way of life. After travelling for nine months across the American continent, he returned home and, in 1835 and 1840, published his famous observations in two volumes titled, *Democracy in America*. Mr. de Tocqueville was fascinated with the expanded political role of the common man in America.

In a chapter titled, "The Principle of the Sovereignty of the People of America," Tocqueville writes, "In America the prin-ciple of the sovereignty of the people is neither barren nor con-cealed, as it is with some other nations....If there is a country in the world where the doctrine of the sovereignty of the people can be fairly appreciated, where it can be studied in its application to the affairs of society, and where its dangers and its advantages may be judged, that country is assuredly America...from their origin, the sovereignty of the people was the fundamental prin-ciple of most of the British colonies in America....[But] ....At the present day, the principle of the sovereignty of the people has ac-quired in the United States all the practical development that the imagination can conceive. It is unencumbered by those fictions that are thrown over it in other countries, and it appears in every possible form...Sometimes the laws are made by the people in a body...and sometimes its representatives, chosen by universal suffrage, transact business in its name and under its immediate supervision...in the United States, there society governs itself for itself....The people reign in the American political world as the Deity does in the universe. They are the cause and the aim of all things; everything comes from them, and everything is absorbed in them." (Bradley 1945, Vol. I, 57-60)

But later Tocqueville tempers this glowing account by pointing out some dangers associated with America's rush toward mass democracy. In a chapter titled, "Government of the Democracy in America," he cautions that, "It is a constant fact that at the present day the ablest men in the United States are rarely placed at the head of affairs; and it must be acknowledged that such has been the result in proportion as democracy has exceeded all its former limits. The race of American statesmen has evidently dwindled most remarkably in the course of the last fifty years....I hold it to be sufficiently demonstrated that universal suffrage is by no means a guarantee of the wisdom of the popular choice. Whatever its advantages may be, this is not one of them." (Bradley 1945, Vol. I, 207, 209)

There is more than a hint here that Madison's hope that civic virtue would fill the government with good men had not been fulfilled. As the founders' original concept of civic virtue faded during this period, some historians suggest it was replaced by a form of social virtue promoted by spreading religious congregations.

In addition to greater participation in electoral politics, citizens enthusiastically formed and joined all sorts of associations, some of which are listed in Table 1. Associations advocating social and political change included the American Antislavery Society, founded in 1833, and the women's rights movement launched in 1848 at Seneca Falls, New York.

Professional groups, including the American Medical Association and the American Institute of Architects, got their start by 1860. Other newly created associations tackled the urgent health and housing problems festering in the slums of rapidly growing cities, including the American Public Health Association and associations of fire and police chiefs.

America's association mania was described by de Tocqueville this way: "Americans of all ages, all conditions, and all dispositions constantly form associations. They have not only commercial and manufacturing companies, in which all take part, but associations of a thousand other kinds, religious, moral, serious, futile, general or restrictive, enormous or diminutive." (Bradley 1945, Vol. II, 114)

* * * * *

The evolving idea of democracy and self-rule got a mid-century boost when Abraham Lincoln, during his famous 1863 Gettysburg Address, said "…we here highly resolve these dead shall not have died in vain; that the nation, shall have a new birth of freedom, and that government of the people by the people for the people, shall not perish from the earth." To this day, school children across the nation memorize these words, and many leave school believing Lincoln's words are an accurate description of the way the American democracy actually works.

TABLE 1
Association Mania

Political Associations
1848   Democratic National Committee
1856   Republican National Committee

Advocacy Associations
1866   American Society for Prevention of Cruelty to Animals
1874   Women's Christian Temperance Union
1909   National Association for the Advancement of
        Colored People

Professional Associations
1847   American Medical Association
1852   American Society of Civil Engineers
1857   American Institute of Architects
1863   American Veterinary Medical Association
1865   American Association of School Administrators
1872   American Public Health Association
1873   International Association of Fire Chiefs
1876   American Library Association
1878   American Bar Association
1880   American Society of Mechanical Engineers

1882   National Funeral Directors Association
1893   International Association of Chiefs of Police
1893   National League for Nursing
1895   National Association of Manufacturers
1897   National Parent Teachers Association
1902   American Road and Transportation Builders Association
        Urban Management Associations
1910   National Urban League

Social Associations
1816   American Bible Society
1819   Independent Order of Odd Fellows
1858   Young Women's Christian Association
1867   Grange
1876   Appalachian Mountain Club
1881   American Association of University Women
1888   National Geographic Society
1892   Sierra Club

A Few Good Citizens Will Do, Again (1880s to 1920s)

By the 1880s, political bosses, machine politics and political patronage had begun to lose much of their appeal and, with it, the
opportunity for many citizens to take a direct role in the operation of their governments narrowed. Government workers supplied by the party-controlled "spoils system" often lacked the
training and skills increasingly needed by public agencies providing ever more sophisticated health, transportation, housing
and community safety services. As party bosses lost their grip on
public jobs, federal, state and city agencies began to hire employees based on their demonstrated ability to perform specific tasks
rather than on their political ties.

If mass democracy for Andrew Jackson literally meant plac-
ing the peoples' hands on the public tiller, in response to a rapidly
changing America, Woodrow Wilson—the Princeton scholar
and future U.S. president—was at the forefront of a movement
to replace untrained, political party appointees with competent
public employees. Unlike Jackson, Wilson declared that the attempt to turn untrained citizens into public employees was getting in the way of, not advancing, the cause of the democracy.

The industrial revolution was in full swing. Big, politically powerful corporations were busy mining ore, drilling for oil, making steel, building railroads and creating self-serving monopolies. And thousands of immigrants flooded into our cities each year creating enormous urban slums. That the nation needed to urgently address these and other emerging social and municipal problems prompted, in the late 1800s, the so-called efficiency movement, a belief that America's future prosperity depended upon the wholesale application of scientific management methods in both public and private organizations.

As large cities replaced small towns, the need for more and better public services skyrocketed, and the services provided by local and state governments required a public workforce filled with engineers, finance, health and education experts. Passage of the federal Pendleton Act in 1883, calling for a merit-based federal civil service workforce, became a public management turning point as state and local governments followed suit and also adopted merit-based hiring practices.

The Interstate Commerce Act of 1887 marked the passage of the United States from a simple agricultural economy into a complex, industrial society with the creation of the Interstate Commerce Commission—a federal agency assigned the task of regulating out-of-control corporations.

Also in 1887, Woodrow Wilson sized-up this hectic period of social and political change with an influential essay in the *Political Science Quarterly*, titled, "The Study of Administration." He called for both more efficient public agencies at all levels of government and a radical change in the relationship between the sovereign American people and their self-rule government.

Madison's original design barred the people from taking a direct role in the operation of the federal government. Jackson reversed course in the mid-1800s by opening the door wide for citizen participation in the governing process. By the late 1800s, however, Wilson was attempting to slam that door shut.

Wilson, echoing Madison, asserted that government by the people was not working, that an elite public corps was needed to make democracy work. Madison wanted a few good men guided by their civic virtues to conduct the public's business. Wilson called for a few good men and women possessing professional skills to manage the public's business.

By the late 1800s, Wilson said, "It is getting harder to run a constitution than to frame one." (Shafritz 1978, 4) More administrative efficiency was needed, he argued, in order to carry out the principles found in the Constitution, not to subvert them. "There is," he wrote, "scarcely a single duty of government which was once simple which is not now complex; government once had but a few masters; it now has scores of masters." (Shafritz 1978, 5)

And, he declared, none other than the founding principle of popular sovereignty of the people was standing in the way of a more efficient government. His claim against citizen involvement in the operation of government went like this: "What, then, is there to prevent? Well, principally, popular sovereignty. It is harder for democracy to organize administration than for monarchy....The very fact that we have realized popular rule in its fullness has made the task of organizing that rule just so much more difficult. In order to make any advance at all we must instruct and persuade a multitudinous monarch called public opinion...An individual sovereign will adopt a simple plan and carry it out directly...But this other sovereign, the people, will have a score of differing opinions." (Shafritz 1978, 8-9)

"The single person who was sovereign," Wilson noted, "was generally either selfish, ignorant, timid, or a fool—albeit there was, now and again, one who was wise. Nowadays the reason is that the many, the people, who are sovereign have no single ear which one can approach, and are selfish, ignorant, timid, stubborn, or foolish with the selfishnesses, the ignorances, the stubbornnesses, the timidities, or the follies of several thousand persons—albeit there are hundreds who are wise." (Shafritz, 1978, 9)

In short, Wilson made the case that to preserve the democratic goals upon which the Constitution was based, efficient public administration must be separated from the inefficiencies associated with popular, self-rule politics.

The central problem, Wilson claimed, was to find the proper role for public opinion—an expression of the people—in the governmental process. That role, he said, should be restricted to an "authoritative critic" of government, not a direct role in the running of the government. In America, he added, the people use the vote to try and do too much and, in the process, produce inefficient government bureaus.

Starting with Wilson, professional public bureaucracies began their slow but steady expansion in America at all levels of government and the role assigned to the people in the American governmental process began a slow, but sure, retreat. Little by little, government of the people, by the people and for the people was being replaced with government rule catering to special interest groups. From this time forward, politicians seldom referred in public speeches to the sovereign people. Voters, yes; citizens, yes; but sovereign, self-rule people, no way.

As the 19th century came to a close, citizen turnout for presidential elections began to decline. After 1908, voter participation never again reached higher than 65% and in many elections the percentages dipped into the 50s and 40s. Desperate economic and social issues needing government attention distracted the nation away from building a self-ruling democracy involving citizen participation.

And during the last half of the 19th century, the influential champion of a society free of government regulation, Herbert Spencer, adapted Charles Darwin's description of nature to justify the free-for-all business practices of America's growing number of politically powerful industrialists. Since the strong beasts justly dominate the natural world, so Spencer argued, governments should not intervene in the business world to protect the weaker members of the human community.

In his famous "Cross of Gold" speech in 1896, William Jennings Bryan pushed back against the world according to Spencer and declared the government must issue money in a way that served the needs of debt-burdened farmers, not to favor banks and owners of capital.

He challenged the rise of America's privileged industrial class and signaled a need for government to intervene. "What we need," Bryan said, "is an Andrew Jackson to stand as Jackson stood, against the encroachment of aggregated wealth....There are two ideas of government. There are those who believe that if you just legislate to make the well-to-do prosperous, that their prosperity will leak through on those below. The democratic idea has been that if you legislate to make the masses prosperous their prosperity will find its way up and through every class that rests upon it." (Bryan 1896)

The Progressive Era

The 20th century opened with a tug-of-war between two views of how the American democracy should work. On one side were those still clinging to the 19th century view that a good, democratic society would somehow well up from the masses below. The contrary view of the Progressive Era reformers, however, sought to replace the earlier populist view of democracy with a radically different kind of citizenship in America.

Believing the future of democracy could not be left to chance, the reformers wanted to replace manipulation-prone and often ill-informed voters of the 19th century with enlightened 20th century citizens. Better-informed citizens equipped with new voter-responsive governing tools and the expansion of professionals in public service could surely meet and solve the complex public challenges facing our industrializing and urbanizing society.

An ambitious set of reforms (see Table 2) sought to enable a cadre of super-citizens to regain control over the political process at all levels of government. The number of public offices to be filled through direct elections increased—dealing a blow to patronage appointments—while, at the same time, reformers tried to create smarter, better informed voters.

If the political bosses tended to the social and economic needs of lower class urban dwellers and effectively mobilized them politically in the past, the progressive reforms had the opposite effect.

Some reforms intended to reduce the influence of political bosses and parties in elections—the secret ballot, for example—actually had the unintended side effect of creating a big decline in voter turnout in elections. Compared to the late 19th century's record breaking voter turnouts for presidential elections, early 20th century reforms tended to ignore and politically demobilize a large slice of the poor and immigrant communities. As the reformers' focus shifted toward management of governing systems, citizens once collectively considered politically the popular sovereign, lost ground in the public systems designed by management experts.

TABLE 2

Progressive Era Reforms

	REFORM	HOPED FOR EFFECT
City Reforms	Replace mayors with city commissions	Limit power of political "machines" and party bosses in city politics and administration
State Reforms	Direct primaries allow voters to select ballot candidates **Initiative:** allow voters to use petitions to place new laws and state constitutional amendments on the ballot. The popular vote then enacts the initiative as a law or rejects it **Referendum:** allow voters, by petition and popular vote, to reject a law passed by the state legislature **Recall:** allow voters, by petition and popular vote, to force an elected official to stand for re-election	Increase government responsiveness to citizens, increase citizen participation in government process, and promote better informed citizens
Federal Reforms	17th Constitutional Amendment: direct election of senators (1913) 19th Constitutional Amendment: women suffrage (1920)	Increase number of eligible voters and direct election to select senators (no longer appointed by state legislatures)

The National Municipal League, founded in 1894, focused on building more efficient city bureaus and modernizing their administrative practices. In 1920, the 19th amendment to the Constitution gave women the right to vote and, in the same year, the League of Women Voters opened for business. By delivering quality information on public issues of the day, League members believed men and women could become better-informed voters as well as more effective participants during election campaigns and in the governing process between elections.

The new 20th century view of effective citizenship in America favored fewer enlightened voters rather than masses of relatively ignorant citizens showing up at the polls. If the common man once felt empowered by 19th century populism, the Progressive Era reforms left millions of less educated citizens out of the political participation loop.

Both 18th century Madison and 20th century Progressive Era reformers seem to be saying that all an effective American democratic republic needs is a few leaders well supplied with civic virtue and a few educated voters—leaving a majority of the citizens to simply stand aside and watch the show.

Governing Without Citizens (Since the 1930s)

Self-rule, the founding idea that individuals are responsible for and possess the mental capabilities and free will to control their own political fate, took another sharp turn during the Great Depression.

At the height of the Depression in 1933, 24.9% of the nation's total work force, 12,830,000 people, were unemployed. Wage income for workers lucky enough to have a job fell 42.5% between 1929 and 1933. Faced with this economic disaster, families split up or migrated from their homes in search of work. "Hoovervilles," shanty towns constructed of packing crates, abandoned cars and other cast-off scraps, sprung up across the nation. Gangs of youths, whose families could no longer support them, rode the rails in boxcars like so many hoboes, hoping to find work. "Okies," victims of the drought and dust storms in the Great Plains, left their farms and headed for California, the new land of "milk and honey." (Franklin D. Roosevelt Library and Museum)

As millions of Americans turned to and became dependent on the government for basic life-support services during the Depression, some observers claim the popular idea that Americans were, in fact, self-governing citizens was lost. Before the 1930s, direct government services were seldom received on a personal level. That changed as the New Deal policies created a fundamentally new relationship between individual citizens and their governments. At the same time, government regulation of the conduct of private businesses expanded greatly.

In Washington, dozens of new federal assistance agencies (see Tables 3 and 4) came into being. As dependence on government services and government regulation of private enterprises increased, so did the political tug-of-war for control over government resources. Citizens, individually and in groups, as well as bankers and industrialists, used politics and the ballot box to achieve economic favors and to win government benefits, rights and entitlements. For decades to come, working class citizens looked to the Democratic Party for the continuation of these personal services while economically better off citizens generally favored Republican Party policies aimed at shrinking the dependence on government services.

While the Depression radically altered the relationship between citizens and their governments, Americans still clung to the traditional, now romantic belief, that they, the people, lived in a self-rule democracy. Professor Robert H. Wiebe, an historian and author of *Self-Rule: A Cultural History of American Democracy*, is one of the best-known sources for tracing the changing role of citizens during the transition from the 19th to the 20th centuries.

If the 19th century united a democratic "people" in the political arena, the efficiency-hungry 20th century, according to Wiebe, gave rise to two powerful forces—the centralization of economic and political power and the rise of bureaucratic corporate and government hierarchies. Both worked to destroy the "We the people" vitality formed in the 19th century and reduce political access and political participation for ordinary citizens.

TABLE 3

New Deal Era Federal Agencies

1932   Reconstruction Finance Corporation

1933   Agricultural Adjustment Administration; Civilian
       Conservation Corps; Commodity Credit Corporation;
       Civil Works Administration; Farm Credit Administration;
       Federal Deposit Insurance Corporation; Home Owners
       Loan Corporation; National Labor Board; Tennessee
       Valley Authority; United States Employment Service;
       Public Works Administration; National Recovery
       Administration; Federal Emergency Relief Agency

1934   Federal Farm Mortgage Corporation; Federal Housing
       Administration; Federal Communications Commission;
       National Railroad Adjustment Board; National Resources
       Board; Securities and Exchange Commission

1935   Social Security Board; National Youth Administration;
       Resettlement Administration; Rural Electrification
       Administration; Works Progress Administration; Railroad
       Retirement Board; Soil Conservation Service; National
       Resources Committee; National Bituminous Coal
       Commission; National Labor Relations Board; Bituminous
       Coal Labor Board

1936   United States Maritime Commission

1937   United States Housing Authority; Farm Security
       Administration

1938   Maritime Labor Board; Temporary National Economic
       Committee; Civil Aeronautics Authority; Federal Crop
       Insurance Corporation

1939   Federal Loan Agency; Federal Security Agency; Federal
       Works Agency; National Resources Planning Board

Industrial and political changes during the late 1800s and early 1900s were closely tied to one another. As the nation industrialized, the wage gap between skilled and unskilled workers grew to a record level by 1916. Opportunities to rise from unskilled to skilled jobs shrank. This lower class labor pool of poor whites, blacks held back by state and local Jim Crow sanctions and ethnic and immigrant minorities filled urban slums, and there they remained politically alienated.

The introduction of the secret ballot in all states by 1891 changed the act of voting from a collective, community act—popularized in the 19th century—into a private act. "By the 1920's," writes Wiebe, "almost no voices spoke up for the old collective, hurly-burly democracy....The cohesive political community, once a democratic ideal, now looked downright ominous in the form of an impenetrable immigrant neighborhood." (Wiebe 1995, 137) The 19th century outpouring of citizens during elections slowed dramatically as lower class citizens dropped out of politics.

Here is how Wiebe sums up the grand shift that transformed the citizen-centric 19th century democracy movement—built on a belief that self-rule was a natural and moral force—into the modern day, interest group dominated politics that pushes individual citizens onto the sidelines. "In the 19th century, the terms 'America' and 'democracy' were practically interchangeable. Citizens assumed they could create democracy without much help from governments." (Wiebe 1995, 181-182)

In fact, a popular 19th century belief equated a limited national government to greater personal liberty. But, as 20th century democracy became more and more defined in individual, not "We the People" terms, all public problems became viewed as national problems requiring national solutions. Democracy itself became more bureaucratized and centralized. In the 19th century, elective politics protected the rights of individuals. In the 20th century, government bureaucracies replaced the ballot box as the trusted defender of the wellbeing of individual citizens.

Wiebe goes on to say that citizens no longer create democracy; they have become beneficiaries of government services. (Wiebe 1995, 218) "The modern individual's growing reliance on government marked a shift with momentous consequences:

TABLE 4

Expanding the Public Policy Arena

	New Deal Actions	Non-Government Policy Actors
Agricultural Adjustment Act 1933, 1938	Farm product price stabilization	Agriculture business and farm operation groups
Federal Emergency Relief Administration 1933, 1935	Aid to states to help destitute individuals	State governments
Emergency Banking Relief Act 1933	Insolvent banks closed	Financial sector groups
Farm Credit Act 1933	Refinance farm mortgages	Lenders and farm operation groups
Glass-Steagall Banking Act 1933	Separate commercial and investment banking	Financial sector groups
Home Owners Loan Act 1933	Aid to home buyers and distressed mortgage holders	Lenders and housing industry groups
National Industrial Recovery Act 1933	Right to organize workers, minimum wage and child labor protection	Labor, business and welfare groups
Federal Communications Act 1934	Establishes Federal Communications	Federal Trade Commission

	New Deal Actions	Non-Government Policy Actors
Federal Housing Act 1934	Mortgage guarantee program for home buyers	Lenders and housing industry groups
National Labor Relations Act 1934	Right to collective bargaining	Labor and business groups
Securities Exchange Act 1934	Regulate stock trading in public corporations	Investment sector groups
Resettlement Act 1935	Aid to farm workers	Farm operators and farm workers
Social Security Act 1935	Old age pensions & unemployment insurance	Various welfare and advocacy groups
Farm Tenancy Act 1937	Aid to poor farmers	Farm operators and farm workers
United States Housing Act 1937	Build public housing	Lenders and housing industry groups
Federal National Mortgage Association 1938	Create secondary mortgages market	Lenders and housing industry groups

Source:
University of California at Berkeley, Department of Geography, "The Living New Deal."

the state replaced the People as democracy's last resort….As the People dissolved, the state thrived." (Wiebe 1995, 202-203)

He concludes with a reminder that the essence of a democracy is citizen participation and that citizen participation requires popular access to the governmental process and a responsive governmental system. Citizens have lost both access to, and responsiveness from, the political system. Powerful interest groups, their lobbyists and professional managers and financiers of political campaigns now rule both the electoral process and policy-making process between elections. Citizens will remain on the outside looking in until the two great constraints on modern democracy—centralization of public and private power in government and corporate hierarchies that resist popular participation—are torn down.

Quoting Eleanor Roosevelt, another historian, Eric Goldman, summed up how the Depression fundamentally changed the relationship between citizens and government: "In the nineteenth century…there was no recognition that the government owed an individual certain things as a right….Now it is accepted that the government has an obligation to guard the rights of an individual so carefully that he never reaches a point at which he needs charity." (Goldman 1956, 288)

"By the 1950s," he says, " the initiative, referendum and recall [important Progressive reforms] had become quaint…The women's vote, in a buzz of activity, continued to make little difference…The process of the atomization of 'the people' into special interest groups had hardly slowed down..." (Goldman 1956, 338)

For still another perspective on how the Depression Era altered the political context of American citizenship, let's turn to another scholar, Theodore Lowi. For our purposes, his central point is that during the 1930s American liberalism, traditionally based on a formal, elected representative form of government providing for law-based public authority, ended. What followed was an interest group liberalism that allowed private interest groups to, in effect, take on the job of formulating public policies. Where elected legislatures once controlled public policy making, during the 1930s the U.S. Congress created a long list of executive branch agencies catering less to the needs of American citizens and more to the needs of well-organized interest groups as they defined what is good for America.

Interest group liberalism, according to Lowi, signaled the passage of American democracy from popular rule. He writes, "The abdication of Congress in the 1930s in the passage of the fundamental New Deal legislation could never have been justified in the name of popular government....The very practices that made convincing use of popular-rule doctrine impossible—delegation of power to administrators, interest representation, outright delegation of power to trade associations, and so on—were what made interest-group liberalism so attractive an alternative....Ultimately direct interest-group participation in government became synonymous with self-government, first for reasons of strategy, then by belief that the two were indeed synonymous." (Lowi 1969, 73, 75)

To sum up, during the New Deal years the role of citizens in the American democracy was altered in two fundamental ways. For the first time in history, the daily lives of citizens became largely dependent on government actions. The public's traditional role—at least in political theory as the popular sovereign—was, in large part, replaced by that of consumer of government services.

In addition, much of the traditional policy making responsibilities vested in government institutions to decide what is good for America and the wellbeing of its citizens was outsourced to self-serving interest groups. Both of these New Deal outcomes have pushed citizens to the political sidelines and have weakened the ability of citizens to play a meaningful role in the governmental process.

21st Century Citizens

For over 200 years, elected officials and leaders of American institutions—including the nation's education systems—have failed to take seriously the promise of a self-rule form of government and have failed to supply Americans with the tools needed to become effective citizens. Perhaps most damning, these leaders and institutions are responsible for shutting citizens out of their own governmental decision making process.

From the start, the rhetoric never fully reflected reality. The image of the sovereign people possessing the ultimate political power amounted to a form of propaganda. Real political power was systematically transferred from the founding 18th century aristocrats to 19th century political party bosses to 20th century government bureaucrats and, finally, to the self-serving interest groups that dominate the who-gets-what policy making process today.

Let's bring our historical survey into the 21st century with the 2004 report titled, *American Democracy in an Age of Rising Inequality*, prepared by the Task Force on Inequality and American Democracy, a study initiated by the American Political Science Association. While the picture presented in this report is disturbing, notice how nicely it fits as the latest chapter in the long, steady decline of the role of American citizens in their self-rule democracy.

"The Declaration of Independence promised that all American citizens would enjoy equal political rights. Nearly every generation has returned to this promise and struggled to elevate the performance of American democracy to its high ideals. But in our time, the promise of American democracy is threatened again....Today, the risk is that rising economic inequality will solidify longstanding disparities in political voice and influence....Our government is becoming less democratic, responsive mainly to the privileged and not a powerful instrument to correct disadvantages or to look out for the majority." (Task Force on Inequity and American Democracy 2004, 18)

"Who Gets the Policies They Want? ...Recent research strikingly documents that the votes of U.S. senators far more closely correspond with the policy preferences of each senator's rich constituents than with the preferences of the senator's less-privileged constituents. Wealthier constituents from the top of the income distribution appear to have had almost three times more influence on their senator's votes than those near the bottom....[and] Government officials who design policy changes are more than twice as responsive to the preferences of the rich as to the preferences of the less affluent." (Task Force on Inequity and American Democracy 2004, 14)

"*Money Buys Attention.* *Today, politicians are not usually directly bribed by political contributors or moneyed interests....What wealthy citizens and moneyed interests do gain from their big contributions is influence over who runs for office and a hearing from politicians and government officials once they are in positions of authority....Money is the oxygen of today's elections...The principal problem is where the money comes from and the influence it buys.*" (Task Force on Inequity and American Democracy 2004, 12)

"*Congress Favors the Organized.* *A century ago the reforms of the Progressive Era aimed to end 'machine' politics that doled out government funds or 'pork' in exchange for votes and campaign contributions. Civil service exams, government oversight, and a more watchful press put a stop to the crudest forms of corruption. But the best-organized still feast on discretionary government spending because members of Congress remain convinced that pork produces votes and campaign contributors.*" (Task Force on Inequity and American Democracy 2004, 13)

"*Renewing American Democracy.* *People are more likely to get involved when they have faith that government can and will address the needs and values of the majority....We challenge our fellow Americans to join with us in a vigorous campaign to expand participation and make government responsive to the many, rather than just the privileged few.*" (Task Force on Inequity and American Democracy 2004, 19-20)

* * * * *

Bottom line—one inequality leads to another in the American political system. Citizens at the lower end of the income ladder are not just poorer, money-wise, than citizens at the top. Those at the top use their greater resources to speak with a much louder political voice, a voice those in positions of political power tend to carefully listen to and respond to.

As the American self-rule experiment unfolded over the past 200 years, not only did America fail to develop the hoped for community-minded civic virtues needed for putting self-rule into practice but, at the same time, public institutions moved in the opposite direction as they created administrative and political systems that actually minimized the need for and the role of citizen involvement.

As government power centralized and interest group politics gained momentum, citizen participation became more and more difficult. The historical trend goes like this:

1. The U.S. Constitution itself set limits on citizen participation. America's representative government abandoned the classical Greek and Roman republican models emphasizing citizen participation. Citizen participation was no longer considered the central requirement in a republican form of government. Instead, Madison's model bet that with a check and balance arrangement among institutions, a few good men could control the destructive forces of special interests. He lost that wager.

2. Next, as suffrage expanded from a few property-owning white men in the early 19th century to nearly all white men and then, finally, all men and women in the 20th century, self-rule responsibilities were spread more widely. But as eligible voters increased in numbers, their political influence proved no match for political access given to powerful interest groups.

3. As governments grew larger, more bureaucratic, complex and run more and more by experts, citizen participation became a burden to public agencies, not an asset.

4. The Progressive era reforms failed to level the political playing field for citizens.

5. New Deal policies turned would-be self-governing citizens into dependent consumers of government services.

6. Finally, in recent decades, as elections and government decisions have become more and more dominated by well-organized and financed interest groups, their paid lobbyists, and wealthy individuals, the influence of voters at the polls and in the policy making process between elections has gone further downhill.

Even the Supreme Court is actively selling out citizens to wealthy corporations. In Citizens United vs. Federal Election Commission, the court in 2010 gave corporations the green light to directly fund political ads to influence election campaigns.

And in 2000, the Supreme Court, not the people, in Bush v. Gore, decided who would become president.

CHAPTER TWO

Schoolbook Democracy

America's school children are woefully unprepared to take their place as informed, engaged citizens...Our system of public education was founded with the twin goals of preparing each generation for the workplace and active citizenship...we have lost sight of educating the citizen in favor of concentrating on preparing the worker."

Charles N. Quigley
Executive Director, Center for Civic Education
(Quigley, 2007)

* * * * *

What is the purpose of public education in America? Is it to instill in future adult citizens a feeling of political power <u>and</u> to ensure they have the tools to exercise that power? Or, is the purpose of civic education to prepare young citizens to be satisfied with a relatively powerless role in their self-rule democracy?

At about age six, upon entering the first grade, future citizens enter the first stage of civic development. For the next 12 years, their knowledge of adult citizenship will consist mainly of lessons found in civic and government studies textbooks. Upon leaving high school armed with this schoolbook version of American democracy, freshly minted adult citizens will then enter the real world of American politics. Let's take a closer look at the textbook version of democracy our freshmen citizens carry from school into the real world of American democracy.

Historically, there has long been the realization that ordinary citizens living in a self-governing democracy would require some form of basic education. In 1787, the same year in which the American Constitution was drafted, Thomas Jefferson wrote to James Madison, saying, "Above all things I hope the education of the common people will be attended to, convinced that on their good sense we may rely with the most security for the preservation of a due degree of liberty." (Jefferson, 1787)

Perhaps Jefferson foresaw the brewing conflict between the revolutionary-era's call for a self-governing people and the limited role assigned to the people with the adoption of the Constitution. Later, in the early 1800s, Jefferson championed a public education system that would, "enable every man to judge for himself what will secure or endanger his freedom." (Jefferson, 1810)

By the 1840s, Horace Mann and other education reformers were gaining traction. Their message: American citizens need a basic elementary education. Free, statewide elementary-level schools did become a reality in 1852 in Massachusetts, in New York in 1853 and in all other states by 1918.

From the beginning, public education was, in part, designed to give each new generation both a common understanding of the nation's founding principles, as well as grounding in what it means to be an American citizen. While the teaching of historical principles has remained much the same, the second goal, preparing kids for their role in the governmental process, has changed dramatically over time.

As the United States industrialized, urbanized and expanded westward in the 1800s, American society became more diverse, as did the civic roles played by its citizens. At first, only white property owning males were allowed to cast election ballots. But over the course of two centuries, as more citizens received the right to directly participate in election campaigns, the civic education of young persons became ever more crucial.

For school children in the 1800s and early 1900s, civic participation may have been mainly a matter of learning how to cast a ballot. For many Americans, this one act satisfied their involvement in self-government. However, in schools today, civic lessons go well beyond calling on students to vote in elections and now call for citizen participation in the governmental process between elections.

As the role of citizens expanded beyond the ballot box, a tension developed. Greater civic participation called for greater access to the political and governmental systems. But, at the same time, the growth of large, professionally staffed political and governmental bureaucracies—and powerful interest groups—tended to push in the opposite direction and to limit meaningful citizen access to the government decision-making process.

Nineteenth century citizens may have been content to limit their civic role to participation in election campaigns. Young citizens today, however, are apt to leave school confident their historically ordained self-governing status and the lessons found in school textbooks fairly describe the way the American democracy awaiting them really works.

Citizen Participation, Then and Now

The idea that self-rule democracy is not a spectator sport, that good citizens ought to play a direct role in the governmental process during and between elections, has developed over the years. While individual citizens are free to define for themselves what the term "citizen participation" means, one scholar defines citizen participation as: "The direct participation of ordinary men and women, in contrast to public and private elites, in policy making...It is to be distinguished from indirect participation, such as interest group membership and voting." (Morrow, 1980 269-270)

Beyond casting a ballot and sitting on a jury, citizens can actively take part in the governing process, by:
• running for office;
• signing a petition;

- writing a letter to public officials voicing one's position on a public issue;
- writing a letter to a newspaper voicing one's position on a public issue;
- supporting a candidate's election campaign by contributing money or working on his or her campaign staff;
- performing volunteer work in a community organization;
- attending a political rally;
- making a public speech;
- writing an article for publication on a political topic;
- joining a reform group.

Most high schools do a good job teaching young students the basic democratic principles and the formal operation of government bureaus at the federal, state and local levels. Most high schools also instruct their students to take an active part in the governmental process.

However, developing both the civic mind-set and specific skills needed to become an active, effective citizen—writing and speaking skills, the desire to closely follow public issues in the media, the feeling that taking part is worthwhile, a deep appreciation for the need to support the common good, etc.—is often the weak link in school curriculums. Without a personal desire and the skills to tackle public issues, effective citizenship is impossible.

What are the Kids Learning in School?
North Carolina
Citizenship training starts early. A fourth grade workbook used in North Carolina in 2009, for example, tells young students: "In addition to rights, citizens have responsibilities...With rights such as freedom of speech comes the responsibility of being an informed citizen...Informed citizens understand the issues and problems that their community, state and nation face....Many North Carolinians take an active part in state and national government. One way they do this is by making their opinions on issues known. They attend government meetings or contact elected officials by mail, e-mail, or phone." (Harcourt School Publishers 2009, 165-166)

New York

Imagine 16- and 17-year-old students seated in a mid-morning government or civics class at East Aurora High School, located in the Town of East Aurora, New York. Their reading assignment includes the following passages from *American Government: Citizenship and Power*, by Christine Barbour and Gerald C. Wright.

"For the British, the source of political power, or sovereignty, lay with the Parliament. Many colonists, on the other hand, believed that the people were the source of all governmental power. In other words, they believed in popular sovereignty. This is why the Declaration of Independence declares that the government receives its power from 'the consent of the governed.' The founders reinforced this vital idea in the Preamble to the Constitution: 'We the People of the United States…establish this Constitution for the United States of America.' We the People hold ultimate political power." (Barbour and Wright 2010, 69)

"The Role of the People: In authoritarian systems, the people are subjects of their government. They possess no rights that protect them from that government…In democracies, by contrast, people are not subjects, but are citizens…with rights as well as obligations…Democratic theory says that power comes from the citizens, who are sovereign." (Barbour and Wright 2010, 15)

"Popular Sovereignty: American democracy is based on Locke's idea of popular sovereignty, the people are the ultimate source of power in the state. That principle is clearly stated in the opening words of the Constitution. 'We the people,' they say, 'do ordain and establish this Constitution for the United States of America.'" (Barbour and Wright 2010, 20)

"Republican Government: Representative government shows the sovereignty of the people. The people have the power to elect representatives. They also have the power to show their approval or disapproval of representatives' decisions when those officials face reelection." (Barbour and Wright 2010, 20)

"Citizenship in Crisis? While most people can participate in government, many of them do not do so. Believers in elite democracy think lack of participation is not important. Elites in business and politics make all the decisions…But some thinkers worry that decreased participation marks a civic crisis in American politics. They see a swing from community-minded citizens of the past to the self-interested citizens Madison worried about….In this view, participating in politics is the price of upholding liberty. If citizens give up this role, authoritarian government can replace the safeguards of democracy. Free citizens will become obedient subjects. To prevent this dire outcome, all citizens must take responsibility for keeping the republic." (Barbour and Wright 2010, 25)

Virginia
Four hundred miles to the south, students at Lake Braddock High School located in Fairfax County, Virginia, are busy digesting passages from their copies of *Government by the People*, by James MacGregor Burns and others, a popular textbook used by advanced high school students. Here is what they are learning.
In a chapter titled, "The Case for Government by the People," the authors promote active citizen participation but do not include hands-on exercises to translate lecture-like presentations into practical learning activities. The discussion goes like this:
The founding generation secured democratic rights and liberty, but, "Passive allegiance to [democratic] ideas and rights is never enough. Every generation must see itself as having a duty to nurture these ideals by actively renewing the community and nation of which it is a part….Our theme in this chapter is simple: Leadership and constitutional structures and protections are important, but an active, committed citizenry that can assume leadership itself is even more important….The answer lies in educating a nation of citizen-leaders who will, regardless of their professional and private ambitions, care about the concerns of the Republic and strive to make democracy work." (Burns 1998, 765)
The American democracy requires both a certain level of faith and skepticism. "It requires faith concerning our common human enterprise, a belief that if people are informed and caring, they can be trusted with their own self-government, and an optimism that when things begin to go wrong, the people can be relied upon to set them right. A healthy democratic skepticism means never trusting any group with too much power." (Burns 1998, 766)

"Thomas Jefferson believed deeply that every government degenerates when it is trusted to its rulers alone. The people themselves, he wrote, are the only safe repositories of government.... Government by the people requires that a healthy and significant segment of the public be attentive, interested, involved and willing, at least on occasion, to criticize wrong-headed or harmful public policies and rally in support of sensible policies, programs and leadership." (Burns 1998, 766)

"When things go wrong in our government, as is often the case, we seldom blame the U.S. Constitution; we revere it too much. Our belief in popular sovereignty makes us reluctant to blame ourselves. And so we blame the only people left—the politicians. And they, wanting to please us, confirm us in our belief that politicians are at fault by pointing fingers at each other." (Burns 1998, 770)

* * * * *

Civics: Responsibilities and Citizenship, by David Saffell, is another high school textbook used at Lake Braddock High School in the early 2000s.

The author uses the Declaration of Independence to underscore the power of citizens. "People create governments to ensure that their natural rights [life, liberty and pursuit of happiness] are protected. If a government does not serve its purpose, the people have a right to abolish it. Then the people have the right and duty to create a new government that will safeguard their security." (Saffell 1998, 44)

Turning to the Constitution, students learn that the preamble's statement—'We the People of the United States...do ordain and establish this Constitution'—"expresses the most important idea behind our government: The people of the United States have the right and the power to govern themselves. They have chosen to place this power in the hands of a government set up by the Constitution. The government depends on the people for its power and exists to serve them." (Saffell 1998, 64) He adds that citizens have certain responsibilities to be informed, to vote and to participate in government. (Saffell 1998, 134)

The Constitution, the text continues, rests on four basic

principles: popular sovereignty, limited government, federalism and the separation of powers. "Sovereignty is the right, or power, to rule. Popular sovereignty means that people <u>should have</u> the right to rule themselves…The Declaration of Independence is really a statement about popular sovereignty. It says that Americans, like English citizens, must be given the right to govern themselves. The same idea is echoed in the 'We the People' phrase with which the Constitution begins. For the writers of the Constitution, however, popular sovereignty was more than just an abstract idea. They designed a government whose actions <u>would always</u> reflect the will of the people. Under the Constitution, the will of the people is expressed most strongly through elections… If elected officials fail to serve the people as they should, they can be removed from office." (Saffell 1998, 87-88)

Do High Schools Build Strong Citizens?

Magruder's American Government has been published and revised annually since 1917. Each edition tells the reader the textbook is "an enduring symbol of the author's faith in American ideals and American institutions." One reviewer claims this text has captured at least 70% of the civics textbook market in American high schools.

According to a recent edition of *Magruder's*, the American Constitution is built on six basic principles, including popular sovereignty, defined as: "In the United States, all political power belongs to the people. The people are sovereign. Popular sovereignty means that people are the only source of governmental power. Government can govern only with the consent of the governed. The principle of popular sovereignty, so boldly proclaimed by the Declaration of Independence, is woven throughout the Constitution. In its very opening words, in the Preamble, the Constitution declares: 'We the People of the United States… do ordain and establish this Constitution for the United States of America.'" (McClenaghan 2003, 65)

Interest groups "provide one of the most effective means by which Americans try to get government to respond to their wants and needs.…our society is a pluralistic one. It is not dominated by any single elite. It is, instead, composed of a number of distinct cultures and groups. Increasingly, the members of various ethnic, racial, religious and other groups compete for, and share in, the exercise of political power in this country....political parties are chiefly interested in winning elections and controlling government. Interest groups are chiefly concerned with controlling or influencing the policies of government" (McClenaghan 2003, 236-237)

* * * * *

High school texts appear to fill students with a feeling of political power. How well is this political optimism translated into power-in-fact once they leave school?

We the People: A Review of U.S. Government and Civics Textbooks, a report prepared by People for the American Way, reviewed 18 government and civics textbooks used in junior and senior high schools throughout the country. The report's stated goal: "To evaluate the texts' capacity to impart to students the knowledge and skills necessary for democratic citizenship, as well as lively enthusiasm for participation....But our reviews agree that many of the books have a common, major deficiency. While they are impressive collections of facts, they are intellectually and pedagogically dull tools for inspiring effective participation in the democratic political process. Many of the books are largely disembodied expositions of principles and facts, lacking the passion of the conflicts that infuse politics and government with meaning and significance." (Carroll and others 1987, iv)

"With few exceptions, the civics texts combine information with exercises and materials for skill development. For example, *Civics: Citizens in Action*, begins with a discussion of what citizenship means and then addresses the individual's role in society, with emphasis on the development of various skills, e.g., analyzing the news and registering to vote. The civics texts differ fundamentally from government texts in their explicit efforts to promote participation in the political process." (Carroll and others 1987, v)

"With a few notable exceptions the government texts fail in several ways to engage students. They fail to adequately demonstrate how the individual can make a difference in this society, and they tend to give short shrift to the important role of public and private interest groups and their influence on government policy. Further, the government texts generally do not urge participation in the political process or indicate how the student can participate. In sharp contrast, with one exception, the reviewers found that the civics texts do challenge the student to solve problems and participate in civic activities." (Carroll and others 1987, v-vi)

Under recommendations, the report urges that, "The overall approach to teaching government in high schools should be changed from merely imparting information to more broadly preparing students to become concerned, active citizens." (Carroll and others 1987, vi)

* * * * *

The Civic Mission of Schools, a 2003 report by the Carnegie Corporation of New York, noted a number of "disturbing trends related to civic engagement among young people...Surveys show that, compared to earlier generations of Americans, today's young people are less interested in political discussion and public issues, more cynical and alienated from formal politics, more materialistic, and less trusting. In 1968, for example, 86 percent of incoming college freshmen claimed that 'developing a meaningful philosophy of life' was a high personal priority. By 2000 this proportion had been cut in half. In 1968, 42 percent of incoming freshmen said that becoming 'well off financially' was a high priority. By 2000, this proportion had risen to 73 percent." (Carnegie Corporation 2003, 18)

Effective approaches to civic education have the following characteristics:

- "A deliberate, intentional focus on civic outcomes such as students' propensity to vote, to join voluntary associations, and to follow the news.
- "Explicit advocacy of civic and political engagement.
- "Active learning opportunities that offer students the chance to engage in discussions of issues and take part in activities that can help put a 'real life' perspective on what is learned in class." (Carnegie Corporation 2003, 21)

What to do? The report concludes: "We do not recommend

renewing stereotypical civics classes…it is important to underscore that teaching only rote facts about dry procedures is un-
likely to benefit students and may actually alienate them from
political participation, including voting." (Carnegie Corporation
2003, 20)

* * * * *

Sharareh Frouzesh Bennett, in a Center for Civic Education paper, takes a look at "…the nature of citizenship as conveyed by
the three most widely used American civics textbooks."[1]

"The chief failing of each text is the inability or unwillingness
to connect the role of participatory citizenship to institutions of
democracy in a fundamentally compelling way. That is, the institutions are described in such a way as to undermine the necessity
of either citizen oversight or public accountability.…Ironically,
by paying lip service to the importance of citizen participation
to American democracy while offering a limited discussion of
the means or reasons for the necessity of citizen participation,
the texts explicitly limit the scope and implicitly the necessity or
value of citizen participation in American democracy." (Bennett
2005, 2-3)

"Though one might hope that the texts would further explore
the complicated relationship between popular sovereignty and
the delegation of that power to government institutions, they do
little more than haplessly repeat these characterizations. Each
text offers coherent and useful descriptions of government institutions and the way in which they operate and (to a lesser extent)
interact with one another, but only manages to supplement the
narratives with repetitive, empty declarations proclaiming citizens as the final source of authority." (Bennett 2005, 4)

"…the texts thoroughly fail to connect active citizenship to
American constitutional democracy. This is especially trouble-
some because the texts are taught not just as an authority on
American government but also as civics texts committed to
outlining the range and scope of citizenship in an institutional

1 *Civic Participation in Government, by J.E. David and P. Fernlund, (2003); American Civics, by
W.H. Hartley and W.S. Vincent, (2003); and, Civics: Responsibilities and Citizenship, by D.C.
Saffell, (1996)*

context. By extending their projects to the latter mission, while offering such limited means or reasons for the necessity of citizen participation, the texts undermine the institutional rationale for active citizenship." (Bennett 2005, 9)

"By paying lip service to the importance of citizen participation to American democracy while offering a deficient and unsatisfactory exploration of the varying modes, and indeed, necessity of citizen participation, the texts limit both the scope and the value of citizen participation in American democracy." (Bennett 2005, 17)

This study's conclusion: "I am suggesting that perhaps the ambivalence to genuine participatory democracy I point to in these textbooks may, in fact, reflect a critical ambivalence in American society about the desirability of encouraging active citizenship universally." (Bennett 2005, 18)

College Textbooks

Since most citizens do not go on to college, high school textbooks will remain the primary source for teaching—or failing to teach—students the public mindset and skills they will need in our self-rule democracy. The following comments on a college-level text are included here to give the reader what I believe to be a more realistic view of the American political system—a view missing in most high school texts.

* * * * *

George C. Edwards, III and others, *Government in America*. This college text is a good example of a more down-to-earth view of the place of citizens in the modern day American government. It's honest, true-to-life presentation of the world awaiting the arrival of young citizens is refreshing. My worry is that cheerleader-like high school texts set the student up for a political culture clash upon leaving school, whereas those young people who make it to college will be better prepared to meet and live in our democracy as it really exists.

Compared to high school government texts, this book is unique. Instead of repeatedly quoting passages from historical documents, it is mainly a description of how the American political system actually works. As an indicator of its focus on the practical, not the theoretical, the term "popular sovereignty" simply does not appear anywhere in its 600 plus pages.

The authors tell us, "We write *Government in America* to provide our readers a better understanding of our fascinating political system…We ask, "What difference does politics make to the policies governments produce?"" (Edwards, and others, 2007, xxv)

The section titled, "Defining Democracy," starts out, "The word democracy is overused…with only positive connotations…Today most Americans would probably say that democracy is 'government by the people.' This phrase, of course, is part of Abraham Lincoln's famous definition of democracy from his Gettysburg Address: 'government of the people, by the people, and for the people.'…The best that can be said of this definition is that it is brief; it is not, however, very informative. The late E.E. Shattschneider claimed that we ought to get rid of confusing language such as 'government by the people.' To say that 250 million Americans 'govern' does not shed much light on the role of people in the American political system." (Edwards, and others, 2007, 11-12)

The realistic worldview found in this text is reflected in these statements.

"Years ago, the power of the few—the elite—might have been based on property holdings. Today, the elite are likely to be those who command knowledge, the experts." (Edwards, and others, 2007 14)

"Individualism remains highly valued in the U.S., with the public policy consequences being a strong preference for free markets and limited government." (Edwards, and others, 2007, 19)

Unlike many high school texts that avoid giving students a realistic appreciation of the political arena awaiting them, here we find a long, evenhanded discussion of the pros and cons of the role of interest groups and how they influence government policies, including profiles of a long list of interest groups at work in the halls of government. To further bring interest groups to life, the authors add an exhaustive list of the techniques interest groups use to influence decision makers—from testifying at hearing to engaging in protests. (Edwards, and others,

2007, 264-289)

In the 2007 version of the text, individual citizen participation is downplayed and students are given guidance on ways they can find interest groups that reflect their views. The basis of good government, as found in this text, is not a 17th century philosophy that government derives its just powers from the people, but that the people will get good government only from one that functions properly.

Political participation is defined as: "All of the activities used by citizens to influence the selection of political leaders or the policies they pursue. The most common, but not the only means of political participation in a democracy is voting. Other means include protests and civil disobedience." (Edwards, and others, 2007, 190)

Why can't this straightforward style of instruction be delivered at the high school level? That would be a giant step toward the development of capable, engaged citizens.

Schoolbook Democracy Wrap Up
It is fair to conclude, based on the content of the high school government and civic textbooks cited here, that American schools adequately stress the three pillars of American citizenship. Many, if not most, young Americans leaving high school and entering the real world of American democracy:

- have a basic understanding of how the three branches of government—the legislatures, courts and government bureaus—work;
- believe, to some degree, that "the people" are, in fact, the legitimate and unquestioned source of the political power upon which the American democracy rests;
- accept, at least in theory, that a self-rule democracy requires active citizen participation beyond occasionally casting ballots at election time.

What schools do not do well, however, is give their students the combative, real world skills active citizens will need to effectively take part in the political and governmental process and the personal conviction to do so. To carry out their schoolbook role, citizens need to carefully research public issues, to feel comfortable speaking out on these issues, to hold elected officials accountable for their performance in office and to effectively organize to challenge groups with which they do not agree. Most students do not learn these skills.

If our schools simply encouraged citizens to limit their civic responsibilities to voting for their representatives in the legislature and then to sit back and passively accept what follows as their democratic fate, their lack of civic skills would not be an issue. But that is not what is happening. The schools are urging young citizens to exercise their popular sovereign role, to get involved in many ways, but then the schools fail to arm them with the necessary tools to carry out these political and civic responsibilities.

A study of how well students are being prepared for citizenship, *A New Engagement? Political Participation, Civic Life and the Changing American Citizen*, concludes there is "...no 'silver bullet' antidote to apathy and disengagement....much of the effort of schools is oriented around civic engagement, rather than political activities. Students are encouraged or required to volunteer in their communities...there is less institutional effort aimed at getting young people *actively involved* in politics...Whatever the cause, the effect may be that young people are being trained in the habits of civic participation but not learning the ropes of political activism—and it appears to be taking a toll." (Zukin and others, 2006, 153-154)

What happens when these "unarmed" citizens meet professionally-staffed interest groups, hardened elected officials skilled in avoiding citizen input and government bureaucracies that do not really welcome citizen involvement? It does not take young citizens long to conclude the public arena is stacked against them, that they are not equipped to perform the way good citizens should.

CHAPTER THREE

The Participation Gap

"The citizen can bring our political and governmental institutions back to life, make them responsive and accountable, and keep them honest. No one else can. The one condition for the rebirth of this nation is a rebirth of individual responsibility."

John Gardner, Founder of Common Cause,
(Gardner 1972, 111)

* * * * *

Are American schools setting kids up to fail as citizens? Let's find out what real-life democracy, the democracy actually experienced by Americans, looks like.

If upon leaving high school the real world of American democracy experienced by young adults did, in fact, mirror their indoctrination in schoolbook democracy, fine. But that is not the case. Instead, citizens have for decades described a wide

gap—let's call it the participation gap—separating what they believe to be their place in the American democracy and the role
actually awaiting them in the real world.

The danger is this: once citizens perceive a big gap between
how they think the democratic process ought to operate and the
way it actually does operate, the legitimacy of America's self-rule
form of government is at risk. Why? Because a healthy democracy depends, for its legitimacy, on a high level of trust among
its citizens. As trust in the way our government works slips away,
faith in democracy itself begins a downward spiral. Does a participation gap exist? If so, how big is it? Let's find out.

* * * * *

Here is what a May, 1999 Hart-Teeter national poll (Hart and
Teeter, 1999) for the Council for Excellence in Government
found:

Question: "One goal that Americans have traditionally considered important is to have a government that is 'of, by, and for the
people' meaning that it involves the people and represents them.
In your opinion, do we have a government today that is 'of, by,
and for the people?'"
Responses: 54% said, "No, government is NOT 'of, by and for the
people.'"

Question: "Some people feel close and connected to government, while others feel more distant and disconnected from
government. How would you describe your own relationship [to
Federal, state and local governments]?"
Responses: 63% fairly or very disconnected from the federal
government. 55% fairly or very disconnected from state government. 46% fairly or very disconnected from local government.

Question: "Let me mention some things that people might think
would make government work better. For each one, please tell
me whether you think that it would be very effective, fairly effective, just somewhat effective, or not very effective in making
government work better."

Responses: 83% said "Teach young people more about government and the importance of getting involved in their communities" would be very or fairly effective. 71% said, "Have people take the time to express their views to elected officials" would be very or fairly effective. 69% said "Reform the campaign finance laws to reduce the influence of special interests" would be very or fairly effective.

Question: "Overall, which is more important for improving government: A) having citizens get more informed and involved, OR, B) having elected officials who inspire people?"
Responses: 52% said "Citizens who are more involved," is more important. 28% said "Officials who inspire people," is more important.

* * * * *

A March 2004 national poll by Peter D. Hart Research Associates conducted for C-SPAN (Hart, 2004) reports that "Many Americans feel that they have lost influence over their own government and are looking for ways to regain control." When asked who has a great deal of influence over decisions made in Washington, D.C.:
• 78% said the president
• 68% said large campaign contributors
• 68% said large corporations
• 56% said lobbyists
• 53% said the media
• 42% said individual members of Congress
• 22% said Congressional staffers
• 20% said the general public

* * * * *

A May 2011 national poll conducted by the Pew Research Center for the People and the Press (Kohut, and others, 2011) found that the working relationship between the sovereign American people and their elected, self-rule governments, is a rocky one to say the least. Seven out of ten citizens:

- claimed elected officials don't care what people like me think (69%)
- say elected officials quickly lose touch with voters back home (72%)
- trust the government in Washington only some of the time or never (70%)

* * * * *

A February 2014 poll by the Pew Research Center (Pew Research Center, 2014) reinforces earlier findings. Just 24% of Americans said they trust the government in Washington always or most of the time, a near historic low.

* * * * *

A September 2014 Gallup poll (Gallup Historical Trends, "Trust in Government") asked, "How much trust and confidence do you have in the American people as a whole when it comes to making judgments under our democratic system about the issues facing our country?" If few Americans say they trust government, this poll found that a respectable majority, 59%, of the responders expressed a "great deal or a fair amount" of trust in themselves. While at first glance 59% looks pretty good, it too is actually an historic low. In a 1976 poll, the same question drew an 86% response.

* * * * *

What do these surveys tell us? First, from the citizens' perspective, there surely is a participation gap in America, and it's big, really big and it's dangerous. A majority of Americans feel disconnected from their government, feel powerless and feel their views are not welcomed.

Once citizens feel their central role in the American democracy is more lip service than real, and that their elected representatives, once in office, can easily forget about 'consent of the governed' and tune out the very folks back home who voted them into office, we have a big problem. Trust in the democracy is at risk.

The participation gap raises other questions, such as "whom do government officials really work for, if politicians are more responsive to the needs of their campaign financial backers and lobbyists than the voters?"

Why the Gap?

For decades, opinion polls have shown a large participation gap separating the American people from their governments. For decades, generations of political scientists have tried to explain why the gap exists and what, if anything, to do about it.

But instead of agreeing on why we have a participation gap, these wise men simply spread the blame in all directions. Your task, as you look over the following pages, is to compare your own experience-based view of why the participation gap exists to the reasons given by the so-called experts. Who, or what, do you blame for the participation gap?

- The citizens?
- The political system?
- Political elites?

Based on your own civic experiences, which of these writers best explains how the American democracy really works. Which explanations make sense and which do not? Which authors do you think most accurately describe the American political system you have experienced?

As you read over the following descriptions of how the American democracy works or fails to work, ask yourself: Where do I currently fit in? Which of these snapshots describes the democracy I am most familiar with?

Blame the Citizens

Many researchers are quick to blame the citizens for failing to make democracy work. Why is this? If researchers start with the assumption, as most appear to do, that the success of our so-called self-rule form of government rests mainly on the performance of its citizens, it is tempting to blame underperforming citizens when things go wrong, to conclude, if only the citizens were to take a more active role, their self-rule democracy would perform swimmingly.

IGNORANT VOTERS

In his 2005 book, *Attention Deficit Democracy,* James Bovard blames the citizens themselves for allowing their democracy to be hijacked by self-serving politicians and interest groups. Instead of keeping the political system working for the public's good, the average American citizen remains blissfully ignorant of the political process, thereby opening the door wide for the election of lying and fear mongering politicians.

Bovard sums up what he calls the "myth of voter competence" this way: "Regardless of how often the candidate withholds information, or how many false claims he emits, no matter how deluded the average voter, and no matter what manipulations occur before and during voting—election results are sacrosanct… Attention deficit democracy lacks the most important check on the abuse of power: an informed citizenry resolutely defending their rights and liberties." (Bovard 2005, 2-3)

IRRATIONAL VOTERS

If citizens prefer to remain blissfully ignorant, are they also irrational? In *The Myth of the Rational Voter: Why Democracies Choose Bad Policies,* economist Bryan Caplan writes, "In theory, democracy is a bulwark against socially harmful policies, but in practice it gives them a safe harbor. How can this paradox be explained? One answer is that the people's 'representatives' have turned the tables on them. Elections might be a weaker deterrent to misconduct than they seem on the surface, making it more important to please special interests than the general public. A second answer, which complements the first, is that voters are deeply ignorant about politics. They do not know who their representatives are, much less what they do. This tempts politicians to pursue personal agendas and sell themselves to donors.

"I offer an alternative story of how democracy fails. The central idea is that voters are worse than ignorant; they are, in a word, irrational—and vote accordingly.…Almost all economists and political scientists now accept that the average citizen's level of political knowledge is extraordinarily low." (Caplan 2007, 2-3)

YES-BUT CITIZENS

Nina Eliasoph, in *Avoiding Politics: How Americans Produce Apathy in Everyday Life*, sought to find out why so many individual citizens who, in private, have a lot to say about politics avoid voicing those views in public. She found that while citizens universally want to perform their citizenship duties, a variety of personal barriers prevent them from doing so.

In surveys and interviews, Eliasoph learned that "all groups shared a belief in the responsible, informed, concerned citizen, active in his or her community....But in practice, this idea called for different styles of interaction..." (Eliasoph 1998, 239)

One group believed the responsible citizen should not talk about issues he or she feels unqualified to discuss. Another group, the "cynics," were "frustrated populists that talked politics incessantly in order to show that they themselves knew that living up to the democratic ideal was impossible within the current political and economic structure." (Eliasoph 1998, 239)

A third group, termed the "volunteers," readily give of their time to help with local problems but "they encouraged one another not to talk about issues that could not be solved simply by local citizens' banding together." (Eliasoph 1998, 239)

Only the final group, the "activists," were motivated by a belief in the democratic ideal that by talking with each other, citizens can become informed and are then in a position to challenge governmental institutions.

WHAT'S-IN-IT-FOR-ME CITIZENS

If the participation gap is not caused by ignorant citizens, irrational citizens or shy citizens, maybe the culprit is self-serving citizens.

Robert E Calvert's essay *Political Realism and the Progressive Degradation of Citizenship: A Quiet Constitutional Crisis* starts this way: "I hope in what follows to show why it is indeed so commonplace in our time to see voters not as citizens but as 'individuals' concerned only with their own economic well-being and, similarly, why it is so easy to describe the American Dream as utterly lacking political content. There should be no comfort in this for any of us." (Calvert 1991, 131)

At the time of the American Revolution, says Calvert, the founders, reflecting Enlightenment Age thinking, "asserted, anxiously if bravely," that if they were to govern themselves, in-dividual citizens must put into practice the so-called "republican virtue"—self-discipline, public spiritedness and a devotion to the public good.

And how did this ideal image of the good, public-spirited citizen morph into today's anti-government, what's-in-it-for-me economic man? The turning point, says Calvert, came during the Progressive era-Great Depression-New Deal years when a more active and efficient government became the last source of the material needs for many desperate people. As citizens began to believe government institutions were the source of everlasting abundance, the economic man was born. Thereafter, talk of civic virtue was replaced with the material-based American Dream.

To some, Herbert Hoover included, the emerging welfare state was nothing but the wholesale buying of votes, the destruction of the freedom, independence and moral fiber of the American people. The image Calvert leaves us with is this: "...the average American is not a citizen, but only a self-interested voter..." (Calvert 1991, 150)

LAZY CITIZENS

And the list grows still longer. If American citizens are not igno-rant, irrational, shy or self-serving, maybe they are simply too lazy to make democracy work.

An ex-president of Harvard University, Derek Bok, starts his book, *The Trouble With Government*, "If there is any persistent theme that emerges from this book, it is that many of the gov-ernment's failings are not primarily the result of scheming politi-cians, incompetent bureaucrats, or selfish interest groups; they have their roots in attitudes and behaviors that are widely shared among the people themselves. Much of the fault, in other words, lies not in Washington but in ourselves." (Bok 2001, 13)

He wonders aloud how much effort Americans are willing to put into making governments work better. Bok says citizens in America have more than enough opportunities to make an im-pact beyond just general elections, including primary contests, initiatives, referenda and opinion polls. In addition, he cites a survey that shows a big decline between 1973 and 1994 in the number of citizens working for a political party; attending a political rally; writing to an elected representative; attending a local government meeting and writing a letter to a newspaper. "What people seem to want," he concludes, "is the power to participate, not the hard work of actually doing so." (Bok 2001, 391)

The result is a vicious cycle: The lack of participation leads to apathy and cynicism and "Apathy and cynicism cause the behavior of government politicians to deteriorate, leading to further cynicism and apathy." (Bok 2001, 417)

Since Bok believes citizen participation is an essential ingredient in a democracy, he offers a number of ideas for getting people more involved. Civic education needs to be improved. Too often schools fail to show students how policy issues impact their lives. Local governments need to build in ways to convert passive individuals into engaged citizens.

But, in the end, he does not sound hopeful: "Few of the reforms that would help make government function better will come about without more active and informed citizen participation. In the end, therefore, people do get the quality of government they deserve. No easy remedies or institutional fixes will cure our discontents as long as so many citizens look upon the State merely as an entity to supply them with services in return for paying taxes." (Bok 2001, 419)

IT'S NOT MY JOB

Perhaps, way down deep, there is another, more fundamental explanation. Could it be that citizens just plain don't want the job?

In *Stealth Democracy*, John R. Hibbing and Elizabeth Theiss-Morse use national surveys and focus groups to expose the "myth of participatory democracy" and show that since American citizens do not care about most policies and do not want greater involvement in the political process, they are happy to turn public decision-making authority over to someone else. Instead of wanting elected officials to be responsive to the citizenry, what Americans really want is for public officials to not feather their own nest while in office.

The conventional wisdom is that Americans distrust public decision makers; they would prefer to rule themselves and favor reforms that would shift decision-making power from elite experts to the people. The authors found just the opposite to be the case.

"The last thing people want is to be more involved in political decision making...Most people have strong feelings on few, if any, of the issues the government needs to address and would much prefer to spend their time in nonpolitical pursuits....the people want to know that their government will become visible, accountable, and representative should they decide such traits are warranted. Until that time, however, most people prefer not to be involved....citizens are usually less concerned with obtaining a policy outcome than with preventing others from using the process to feather their own nests....People do not want responsiveness and accountability in government; they want responsiveness and accountability to be unnecessary." (Hibbing and Theiss-Morse 2002, 1-5)

The authors conclude, "The ideal form of government, in the opinion of many people, is one in which they can defer virtually all political decisions to government officials but at the same time trust those officials to be in touch with the American people and to act in the interest of those people and not themselves." (Hibbing and Theiss-Morse 2002, 159)

GIVE US FREEDOM, NOT RESPONSIBILITY

Michael Sandel's take on the state of democracy in America, *Democracy's Discontent: America in Search of a Public Philosophy*, hits on a now familiar theme: while self-rule demands that citizens take an active part in the governmental process, Americans prefer personal freedoms, not community responsibilities.

During the 19th century, says Sandel, public speeches and political actions attempted to instill civic virtues and character in citizens. "By the second half of the 20th century, Americans argued instead about what rights would enable persons to choose their own values and ends." (Sandel 1996, 279)

WHO NEEDS THE PEOPLE?

In *Downsizing Democracy* we learn that for 200 years, ordinary citizens in America were important actors on the political stage, the backbone of the country. However, the authors Matthew A. Crenson and Benjamin Ginsberg tell us, "The era of the citizen is now coming to an end. Today, Western governments have found ways of raising armies, collecting taxes, and administering programs that do not require much involvement on the part of ordinary citizens. This underlying development has, in turn, opened the way for political elites to reduce their dependence upon popular political participation....contemporary political elites have substantially marginalized the American mass electorate and have come to rely more and more on the courts and the bureaucracy to get what they want." (Crenson and Ginsberg 2002, x)

Examples: In the legal struggle over who would receive Florida's decisive presidential electoral votes in 2000, the writers conclude that Al Gore understood the minimal role for citizens in the contest and quote him saying, "I'm quite sure that [public opinion doesn't] matter in this, because it's a legal question." (Crenson and Ginsberg 2002, xi) Instead of involving the people in the election of a president, a few hundred, at most a few thousand, political leaders and activists determined who would gain the White House.

"Just how truncated the role of the ordinary citizen has become in America was patently clear when President George W. Bush called Americans to action in the wake of the 9-11 terrorist attacks on New York and Washington. Did the president ask Americans to sacrifice, to buy bonds, to volunteer for military service or to donate blood? Not exactly. The president told Americans the best thing they could do for their country would be to shop more while the government went about the business of fighting terrorism." (Crenson and Ginsberg 2002, 2)

The book's final sentence reads: "Today, however, the vitality of the public as a force in American politics is crumbling, and the time may soon arrive when the most pressing and yet disturbing question in American politics is 'Who cares?'" (Crenson and Ginsberg 2002, 244)

Blame the Political System

One way to get citizens off the hook is to blame a faceless, nameless political system. Do Americans really want to get involved but, for one reasons or another, are pushed aside? Is the political system purposefully designed to limit citizen participation?

Blame the system advocates, like their blame-the-citizen colleagues, assume that citizens ought to have a more active role in the governmental process. But, rather than directly blaming the citizen, they find that outside forces block the citizen's way into the public arena.

POWER HUNGRY POLITICAL PARTIES

A former member of Congress from Oklahoma, Mickey Edwards, in his book, *The Parties Versus the People: How to Turn Republicans and Democrats into Americans*, tells us political parties no longer empower or serve the citizens of America. Rather, they have become self-serving organizations with little regard for the betterment of the people and the country. "When the pursuit of political power becomes the end-all goal and not merely a tool for achieving a better society, it is democracy itself that is laid beneath the guillotine's blade." (Edwards 2012, 32)

Once formed to deliver good government, American political parties have become rival ideological camps in pursuit of power. By promoting candidates with extreme views, party-controlled primaries perpetuate this inter-party rivalry. Edwards says that to add insult to injury, it is we, the people, through our taxes, who pay for the parties to limit our choices at the ballot box.

Edwards proposes a number of changes to limit the power of political parties and return power to the people, including open primaries in which every candidate for an office, regardless of party, appears on a single primary ballot. All registered voters, regardless of party affiliation, not party bosses, select the top two vote-getters to run against one another in the general election.

The last line in this book reads: "I began this book by talking of you as a citizen, not a subject. As a citizen, take back your democracy. End partisan rule. Do it now." (Edwards 2012, 181)

PROFESSIONALIZATION OF CIVIC LIFE

Once upon a time, according to Theda Skocpol in *Diminished Democracy: From Membership to Management in American Civic Life*, citizens were active in a wide range of civic organizations. This is no longer the case.

For about 100 years, from the mid-1800s to the mid-1900s, cross-class voluntary federations flourished, including: Modern Woodmen of America; Loyal Order of the Moose; the Masons; the Grange; the General Federation of Women's Clubs and the Elks. Through local chapters, these organizations and many more like them, says Skocpol, once fostered citizenship and civic virtue within the general population.

But following the social movements of the 1960s and 1970s, membership organizations shrank. And what took their place? National public life is now dominated by professionally managed advocacy groups—such as political action committees; think tanks; foundations; Common Cause; the Sierra Club; the Children's Defense Fund—that speak <u>on behalf of</u> their constituents and active local chapters are no longer the rule.

The professionally managed organizations that dominate American civic life today are, in important respects, less democratic and far less participatory than the pre-1960 membership federations they displaced. (Skocpol 2003, 7, 13)

POLARIZED POLITICAL PARTIES

America's two party system, in theory at least, is designed to give the citizens access to intelligent debates from different points of view, forums that actually inform voters on important issues of the day. But that is not what *Washington Post* columnist E.J. Dionne, Jr., describes in *Why Americans Hate Politics*.

Real debate on public issues, says Dionne, has been shut down by the rise of polarized politics and symbolic issues. Instead of offering a forum for an honest debate on the proper size of government, whether to raise taxes, or to establish business regulations, etc., leaders in both American political parties use slogans to cling to old, rigid positions on these issues.

"Simply put, conservatives highlight the government's role in promoting individual virtue but downplay the government's responsibility to create a society in which virtue can flourish. Liberals are wary of regulating personal behavior, but would give government a powerful say over the shape of social and economic life." (Dionne 1991, 324-5)

Political elites prefer snappy sound bites that fail to address the complex views held by voters. "Our current political dialogue," he writes, "fails us and leads us to hate politics because it insists on stifling yes/no, either/or approaches that ignore the elements that must come together to create a successful and democratic civic culture…A nation that hates politics will not long thrive as a democracy." (Dionne 1991, 354-5)

CITIZENS LACK REAL POWER

If civic and political life has become overly professionalized and polarized, how about Madison's faith in representative government as the main means for citizens to exercise self-rule?

Voters have the power to elect candidates, but once in office these representatives pretty much hold all the cards. That's the message of Robert J. Pranger's *The Eclipse of Citizenship: Power and Participation in Contemporary Politics*. He divides politics into two parts: the politics of power (the actions of leaders, activists and elites) and the popular politics of citizen participation. The two parts are engaged in an ongoing, lopsided tug-of-war.

The politics of power, in the form of representative government, is rooted in a medieval concept, plena potestas, which gives the elected representative full authorization to act in place of, and bind, his or her constituents. Pranger contends this ancient tradition protects political decisions from citizen involvement, leaving citizens listless, watching from the sidelines. And, as society has become more and more complex and dependent on experts, citizen participation has eroded further and with it, the notion that citizens can, in fact, govern themselves.

"The citizen becomes steadily more restricted in his options for participation...As a consequence, civic virtue declines... Young people learn quite early that certain representative offices provide keys to the entire political structure, and this early awareness probably tends to support later habits of obedience and veneration." But, "the idea of a final say held by the voting public applies only to individual candidates, not to their offices or to the structure of power." (Pranger 1968, 14-15)

INTEREST GROUPS TRUMP CITIZENS

Not officially part of our governmental system, interest groups function as if they were and, in the process, they push citizen participation to the sidelines.

Robert Dahl starts off *Democracy and its Critics* this way: "From ancient times some people have conceived of a political system in which the members regard one another as political equals, are collectively sovereign, and possess all the capacities, resources and institutions they need in order to govern themselves."(Dahl 1989, 1) But as this simple political system, with the citizen at its center, is applied to nation states today, a complex array of associations and interest groups, not the citizens, define the public good.

Dahl argues that citizen participation ought to be brought back into the governmental process in large-scale democracies based on the fundamental belief that all persons ought to be considered equal in some important sense when a society is making collective decisions. Yes, says Dahl, there are inequities in all political systems. But, in the future, institutions should be built to afford citizens voting equality, effective participation, enlightened understanding and some control of the political agenda.

DEMOCRACY SIMPLY DOES NOT EXIST—ANYWHERE

Finally, let's take a look at how Ferdinand Lundberg dashes any notion that democracy is, in fact, found, anywhere. In *The Myth of Democracy*, Lundberg declares: "Democracy is the flaming watchword of the age....Yet it nowhere exists—or ever existed— in the sense that a given government is either 'by the people' or clearly 'for the people' although it is always 'of the people.'" (Lundberg 1989, 7)

So, in what sense does democracy exist? Lundberg looks to the Constitution for an answer and finds that the Constitution set up a system of government that is part democracy and part republic: "Democracy ends where a Federal election ends, and at that point republican government takes over...the election returns decide one outcome and subsequent government actions have an outcome either greatly at variance or diametrically opposed to the electoral mandate." (Lundberg 1989, 52-53)

Elections and subsequent government actions may have little in common, says Lundberg, because elected officials don't really represent the people who voted them into office. He writes, "People often say 'their' congressman or senator is 'their' representative. But, constitutionally, these officials are representatives of a congressional district or state, not of the members of that state or district, individually or collectively... any idea of an indirect democracy at work seeking to advance the individual interests of the citizens, is completely out of the question." (Lundberg 1989, 120-121)

Blame the Elites

If neither the political system nor the citizens themselves are at fault, what is the role of that elite corps that readily fills any civic void? Madison speculated that the American democracy would prosper with a few virtuous, elected representatives carefully chosen by the people. In effect, he designed a form of government that was to be run by the few, not the many. Today a few top government decision makers, lobbyists, powerful individuals and interest groups—the so-called elites—are vilified for the excessive control they exercise in the American governmental system.

THE BETTER INFORMED SHOULD RULE

Because issues are not settled at the ballot box, Roger Cobb and Charles Elder, in their book, *Participation in American Politics: the Dynamics of Agenda-Building*, argue that a healthy democracy must provide for the continued participation of citizens in politics between elections, as legislative agendas are developed and acted upon. Ongoing citizen involvement would help politicians decide which issues should top their agendas and how the issues should be resolved.

But, since the general public is often not well informed and not engaged in the public agenda-setting arena—echoing Crenson and Ginsberg—the authors conclude America has adopted, instead, an elitist form of democracy in which a few individuals, promoting personal interests in the outcome of specific public issues, dominate the governmental process.

ELITISM IS HARDLY NEW

Not all writers consider the rise of political elites to be a recent development. Peter Bachrach's book, *The Theory of Democratic Elitism: A Critique*, contends the American system is driven by a longstanding struggle between classical liberalism (freedom from government meddling in one's life) and democracy (freedom to participate in the public decisions affecting one's life). From the 1770s to the 1940s, according to Bachrach, liberalism and democracy were easily reconciled.

But with the rise of communism around the globe and America's own radical reaction to totalitarian threats, the long assumed attachment of the common man to personal liberty was dashed. A strong state, like it or not, seemed needed to meet these threats. "This," says Bachrach, "is the chief reason for the radical shift in democratic thought in the postwar (WWII) period…. that the great majority of people have a surprisingly weak commitment to democratic values." (Bachrach 1967, 30-31)

This recent rise of elite power has, in the minds of many, rendered obsolete the idea that through political participation citizens can fulfill their self-rule role, and that to cling to this out-of-date ideal will only generate cynicism in the masses as the gap between the democratic ideals and reality widens.

Bachrach sums up this historic shift in the relationship between the masses and the elites this way: "It is the common man, not the elite, who is chiefly suspected of endangering freedom, and it is the elite, not the common man, who is looked upon as the chief guardian of the system….the emphasis is no longer upon extending or strengthening democracy, but upon stabilizing the established system. The focus, in short, is upon protecting liberalism from the excesses of democracy rather than upon utilizing liberal means to progress toward realization of democratic ideals." (Bachrach 1967, 32)

As for the state of American democracy, he says, "The crucial issue of democracy is not the composition of the elite…Instead the issue is whether democracy can diffuse power sufficiently throughout society to inculcate among people of all walks of life a justifiable feeling that they have the power to participate in decisions which affect themselves and the common life of the community." (Bachrach 1967, 92)

The book ends with this passage: "If it is time to abandon the myth of the common man's allegiance to democracy, it is also time that elites in general and political scientists in particular recognize that without the common man's active support, liberty cannot be preserved over the long run. Democracy can best be assured of survival by enlisting the people's support in a continual effort to make democracy meaningful in the lives of all men." (Bachrach 1967, 106)

LEGISLATURES WORK JUST FINE

James Madison feared the common man's involvement in the legislative process would lead to mob rule. That's also the message in

Alan Rosenthal's book, *The Decline of Representative Democracy: Process, Participation and Power in State Legislatures*. He writes, "Despite the popular perceptions that legislatures are autocratic, arbitrary, isolated, unresponsive, and up for sale, legislatures are in fact extraordinarily democratic institutions. They have been becoming more democratic of late, so that a systemic shift from representative democracy to participatory democracy now seems to be under way." (Rosenthal 1988, x)

One strength of state legislatures, he says, is that they are genuine deliberative bodies where, "More of a premium is placed on information, reason, commonality of interests, and even far-sightedness than is the case in public judgments recorded by a poll or a referendum. Citizens are extraordinarily weak when it comes to deliberation. They are constrained by time, competing interests for whatever leisure hours they have...They have non-attitudes and pseudo-opinions, with answers to questions invented on the spot." (Rosenthal 1988, 41)

Why, then, is there a decline in representative democracy in the states? Rosenthal finds that: "Some of the democratic changes that have come about are salutary, but some of them—especially if carried too far—endanger the legislature's ability to function in a representative and authoritative capacity. The dangers of democracy are already upon legislatures; they are real, and not merely hypothetical." (Rosenthal 1988, 331)

He goes on to list these specific dangers:

Danger of Manipulation. When citizens mobilize on an issue, this can cause elected officials to fear retaliation if their vote does not support the citizens' viewpoint. Lobbyists are less likely to mislead a legislator.

Danger of Less Deliberation. "An excess of public participation hamstrings deliberation...lawmakers are becoming, if not slaves to public opinion, then prisoners of public sentiment." (Rosenthal 1988, 335)

Danger of a Weak Political Institution. "One effect of democratization is the disinstitutionalization of the legislature. No longer are legislatures bounded from their environments, and no longer do they have control over their own internal affairs. The press has intruded into matters that had previously been left to legislatures to manage for themselves. Now the press, and presumably the public, want things done their way. Legislators are reluctant to travel out of state, hesitant to socialize with lobbyists, and fearful that their ethics will be impugned." (Rosenthal 1988, 336)

What to do? "The problem is that the public is completely disconnected from an understanding or appreciation of the political process…Ordinary people cannot appreciate such a chaotic process or bizarre form of life….much more is required if citizens are to become familiar with the institutions of representative democracy." (Rosenthal 1988, 342-343)

Rosenthal's final paragraph reads: "Legislatures have lived up to their end of the bargain with the public. It is time for the public to live up to its end. Otherwise, representative democracy, which has served us well for quite a while, will fade further away." (Rosenthal 1988, 344)

Final Thoughts

Do these writers help us pin down THE cause for America's citizen participation gap? Not really. First, the sheer variety of participation barriers identified by the authors suggests they are observing the visible symptoms of a hidden root problem. While each writer musters enough evidence to support his or her favored malady, there is no way to sort out major from minor breakdowns. Each writer wants the reader to think his or her particular research has uncovered the core problem facing our democracy. Common sense tells us all of the authors can't, simultaneously, be dealing with THE root cause of poor citizen participation.

What we are looking for is not simply to better understand the symptoms associated with citizen passivity but, more importantly, we want to zero in on the source of the various symptoms. OK, let's grant that many citizens don't want to do the hard work required of an effective citizen. But why is this so? Others, understandably, feel unqualified to get actively involved in their self-rule governmental process. But what we want to know is, why?

No doubt about it, American institutions are not built to encourage citizen participation. But why should this be the case? And why is it so easy for elected officials to ignore the very voters that put them into office? Why do policy makers depend more on organized interest groups than on citizens?

Finally, it is one thing to show that the so-called elites have hijacked democracy, but quite another to uncover the underlying reason why so many citizens readily submit to be ruled by the few.

My point is simply this: each writer offers important insights into the outward actions of citizens, political systems and elite actors. What they don't do, however, is uncover the fundamental, underlying forces that produce these visible manifestations in citizens, systems and elites. More on that in the next chapter. For now, before you go on to Chapter 4, clarify in your mind which of the above symptoms you think best explains your own reluctance to become a more engaged citizen. The polls are clear. There is a democratic participation gap in America. However, since the experts can't agree on what your role in the democracy ought to be, it is up to you to decide what citizenship means to you and what your level of participation ought to be. In the end, you are free to take an active role or no role at all.

While the wise men quoted here are quick to study and ponder the more visible barriers to citizen participation, the search for answers can't end there. Whatever the reason Americans find themselves on the outside of their democracy looking in, what will they do about it? Where you place the blame for your feeling of powerlessness is the important step toward finding the citizenship style that will work best for you.

In the next chapter we'll dig deeper, looking beyond the blame game and symptoms and try to identify a more fundamental reason so many Americans feel politically abandoned. We'll find that many Americans—including yourself, perhaps—adopt a strange response when confronted with a feeling of political powerlessness. Instead of becoming more active, instead of claiming their rightful role, they tell themselves—contrary to their own established reality—that they are, in fact, in charge of the American democracy. Their beliefs in political myths tell them that all is OK, even as their personal experiences tell a different story.

CHAPTER FOUR

Political Myths

"Nothing is more surprising to those who consider human affairs with a philosophical eye, than to see the easiness with which the many are governed by the few; and to observe the implicit submission with which men resign their own sentiments and passions to those of their rulers. When we enquire by what means this wonder is brought about, we shall find that as force is always on the side of the governed, the governors have nothing to support them but opinion. Tis, therefore, on opinion only that government is founded; and this maxim extends to the most despotic and most military governments, as well as to the most free and popular."

David Hume
Of the First Principles of Government
(Hume 1758)

* * * * *

Because political myths are underreported in newspapers and newscasts, much of what follows may seem new and even wacky. Scholars tend to shy away from giving political myths the attention they deserve. In my view, this is unfortunate, since the American democracy makes little sense in their absence.

Importantly, myths are a reflection of how we, as a nation, look at ourselves and, individually, how we shape our political beliefs and our civic behaviors. All I ask is that you try to proceed with an open mind as we explore the hidden, but powerful, role myths play in the life of American citizens.

The polls cited in Chapter 3 show that most Americans know their democracy is largely a fiction, that the supreme political powers assigned to them in historical documents and in current political speeches simply do not exist in reality. But instead of going to work to defictionalize the American democracy, most Americans play along with the fantasy. In other words, citizens in the world's most celebrated democracy not only roll over and quietly accept politically powerless roles, but their inaction actually works to destroy the self-rule government they believe is theirs.

Let's take a closer look at how Americans have willingly accepted political marginalization and get a better understanding of how political myths are used to reconcile the ideal schoolbook democracy with political reality in America.

WHAT IS A MYTH?
Myths are an important part of our daily lives. There are religious myths, historical myths, children's myths, etc. What we really want to know, however, is how democratic myths play out in the American political system. For starters, let's look at a couple of definitions.

"Historical myths can best be understood as a series of *false beliefs* about America's past. They are false beliefs, however, that have been accepted as true and acted upon as real, and in that acting they have acquired truth. Therefore, myths remain both true and false simultaneously." (Gerster and Cords 1997, xi)

"Myths are stories...they are 'the way things are' as people in a particular society believe them to be...Myths are the patterns—of behavior, of belief, and of perception—which people have in common. Myths are not deliberately, or necessarily consciously, fictitious. They provide good, 'workable' ways by which the contradictions in society…are reconciled, smoothed over, or at least made manageable and tolerable…They are sometimes based on faith, on belief rather than reason, on ideals rather than realities." (Robertson 1980, xv)

Robertson adds, "Very often, the problem being 'solved' by a myth is a contradiction or a paradox, something which is beyond the power of reason or rational logic to resolve." (Robertson 1980, 6)

THE UNITED CITIZENS MYTH

The United Citizens Myth fuels the belief that in a democracy citizens, and their governments, are all bound to one another, all sharing a single understanding of their collective life together. In fact, a wide difference of opinion exists among citizens. The question is, just how united, or disunited, are American citizens?

A long list of scholars has hammered away at this fundamental question. In slightly different ways they arrive at a similar answer. In theory Americans are a politically united, civic-minded people but, in practice, they behave more like self-centered, self-serving individuals. Here are a few snapshots that demonstrate how this political contradiction got started and why it goes on and on.

A Powerful Political Fiction. James Morone, author of *The Democratic Wish: Popular Participation and the Limits of American Government (Revised Edition)*, says our self-image of "a single, united people, bound together by consensus over the public good which is discerned through direct citizen participation in community settings…" is a "democratic myth," a "powerful political fiction." (Morone 1990, 7)

The revolutionary period in American history, 1776-1780s, gave birth to the "democratic wish," that Americans would be a united, virtuous people pursuing a shared public goal through direct participation and subordinating personal, private interests to the common good. But the new government created shortly thereafter with the adoption of the American Constitution in 1789, is rooted in a suspicion, a dread of powerful governments and a deep desire for individual freedom from government meddling and the right to advance one's own, private interests.

Americans throughout history might have wished for a united people with agreed upon public goals promoted by an active government, but their inherited, historical fear of strong governments has, for 200 years, kept the wish just that: an unattainable dream. Since the 1950s, says Morone, a majority of the Americans have supported government-backed attempts to reform health care, but private health care interest groups have successfully limited the role of governments in the provision of health care services.

In the end, Morone concludes: "The democratic ideals that inspire reformers are, like any myth, unattainable," (Morone 1990, 23) rendering 'the people' a powerful fiction. (Morone 1990, 7) What to do? His prescription: Stop kidding ourselves about the fictional role of "the people."

Make-believe Democracy. Way back in 1957, Roscoe Martin, in a book titled, *Grass Roots*, debunked the fiction that the people have turned their backs on democracy. He wrote: "To attribute the supposed decadence of democracy to voter apathy, as is done regularly by most speakers and many writers on democracy, is to mistake effect and cause. The quiescence of the voters is not a cause of the fancied decline of democracy, but a result...Pro forma elections, hollow campaigns, manufactured issues, artificial candidates—this is the world of make-believe democracy in which the citizen is expected to accept fantasy as fact. That he refuses to do this, and oftentimes he 'takes a walk' on election day, is to be attributed more to his good judgment than to his apathy. He fails to vote not because he is delinquent but because politics, and more largely government, has ceased to have significant meaning for him." (Martin 1957, 91)

WHY THIS MYTH ENDURES
Two very different explanations for the staying power of the civic-minded citizens myth are out there. One claims it is simply a case of misunderstanding, that the Constitution never intended to give citizens the central role upon which the myth is based. The other explanation contends that both views—citizens as central players in the democratic process and citizens largely excluded from that process—are necessary, though contradictory, parts of

the American form of government.

E.E. Schattschneider's book, *The Semi-Sovereign People: A Realist's View of Democracy in America*, claims the original idea behind American democracy was not intended to give the people the supreme political power. Instead, for the first time in history, the American democracy created a political tool for use by the people to counterbalance the wielders of economic power. Historically, the economically powerful class also held political power and thereby controlled the political agenda. In the American system, says Schattschneider, from the beginning, sovereignty was divided. Part was given to the people, via their election of members to the House of Representatives, and another part, in a capitalistic economy, was vested in the business community.

But this division of power has been distorted over time. "For more than a century," he says, "we have been giving the government to the people until the people have come to believe us; to think that they own it. The public no longer identifies itself with the House of Representatives as its special agency in the government, as it ought to in constitutional theory. Americans now think that their title covers the whole government, lock, stock and barrel, not merely a piece of it." (Schattschneider 1960, 115)

To keep the notion of democratic popular sovereignty alive, says Schattschneider, "It was necessary to invent the myth that the people seized all power at the time of the American Revolution." (Schattschneider 1960, 121) This ancient view of democracy always assumed—wrongly, as it turns out—the people would take control of public affairs. Nonetheless, it is this erroneous definition of democracy, of the all-powerful people, that is, says Schattschneider, "perpetuated in the textbooks and govern our thinking in the entire area." (Schattschneider 1960, 130)

"The image implicit in the schoolbook definition of democracy is that of a mass of people who think about politics the way a United States senator might think about it....The great difficulty here concerns the assumptions made about the role of the people in a democracy...that the people really do decide what the government does on something like a day-to-day basis.... We become cynical about democracy because the public does not act the way the simplistic definition of democracy says it should act, or we try to whip the public into doing things it does not want to do, is unable to do and has too much sense to do." (Schattschneider 1960, 133-135)

Until a more honest definition replaces the schoolbook definition, until we define the role of the people as it really exists in the American democracy, the distrust of government will continue. Schattschneider ends with what he calls an operational definition of democracy: "Democracy is a political system in which the people have a choice among alternatives created by competing political organizations and leaders. The advantage of this definition over the traditional definition is that it describes something that actually happens." (Schattschneider 1960, 141)

In *The American Political System: Ideology and Myth*, Mark Roelofs and Gerald Houseman contend that two legitimate, but contradictory, political ideas—myth and ideology—both prosper in the American democracy. The book starts with this question: "Why does our political life so often appear to be quite different from what it really is?" (Roelofs and Houseman 1983, 1)

We appear, the authors tell us, to live in a real democracy. But, "…whereas it is in every appearance a true democracy, in practice it falls short of the ideal many times in many ways. National slogans about the 'sovereignty of the people,' patriotic songs about this 'sweet land of liberty,' monuments to fallen heroes such as Abraham Lincoln and, above all, the unceasing rhetoric of our politicians during their extended and expensive campaigns all seek to persuade us that our government is truly of, by, and for the people." (Roelofs and Houseman 1983, 1)

According to the authors, "Myth is our national hope. It is what we are taught to believe about ourselves and our government by slogan, song, and saga, but also by folk wisdom, school texts and teachers, and the customs and values implicit in a host of citizenship activities. The most important of these activities, incidentally, is voting in national, state and local elections…By believing myth, by believing our government to be in conscientious service to certain ideals, and by accepting it for what it appears to be in myth, we prepare ourselves to obey its laws and to support it with our loyalty, our taxes, and, if need be, our lives." (Roelofs and Houseman 1983, 2-3)

In short, these myths—including sovereignty of the people,

separation of powers in the Constitution and a responsible two party government—create and legitimize, in our minds at least, what makes America, America.

On the other hand, "Ideology comprises the practical institutions, [examples being the courts and state governments], understandings, assumptions, and values by which authority and authority relationships are established, operated and maintained.... relationships about who is to do what, how, why and to whom... Ideology is concerned with persuasion, influence, brokerage, job-seeking, power and coercion." (Roelofs and Houseman 1983, 3)

"In a profound sense", they write, "the system gives every appearance and promise of being a Social Democracy pursuing broad goals of community solidarity, justice and equality...It is equally true, however, that behind its sincere appearance and constant promise, the system operates by paying attention to very different ideas. Success is to the strong and well connected; government is cliquish and elitist. The system is representative but mostly heeds the clashing and persuasive claims of vested interests." (Roelofs and Houseman 1983, 31-32)

This paradox can exist, they conclude, because our political myths define how most Americans believe their governments ought to operate, while the same Americans also accept the manner in which they actually operate. The myths and the reality are two parts of a single whole and do not exist independently of one another.

And how do these two conflicting parts of the American system BOTH gain legitimacy generation after generation? Each generation of citizens confers legitimacy by repeatedly acknowledging the existence of both the idealized version of democracy contained in myths and the way government actually works. Myths are routinized and learned by rote in songs and speeches and symbolized in monuments. Only then do they become "national mythic traditions." And the nation's granddaddy national mythic tradition is simply that America is a single, united people with a system of popular government.

Reinforced with frequent popular elections, this cornerstone myth is accepted as fact, generation after generation. In this way, citizens legitimize the real-life democracy operating in America today, a governmental system in which they are largely powerless.

The Popular Sovereign Myth

Perhaps no one has done a better job tracing the origins of the popular sovereign myth than Yale professor Edmund Morgan. The absolute power of English monarchs had long been eroding when, during the period 1640 to 1689, members of the British parliament finally managed to outwit the sovereign king with a sovereignty of their own. According to Morgan, an old fiction that heretical kings ruled with divine authority was replaced with a new fiction that the elected parliament ruled with the sovereign authority rooted, by nature, in the people who elected them.

Parliament's argument went like this: members of the English parliament were, in fact, independently elected to represent the people living in small geographic regions, not the nation as a whole. However, if the parliament, as a single whole body, was to successfully replace the divinely-backed national monarch, it needed an equally powerful sovereignty of its own. Yes, individual members of parliament were elected by a small, local slice of the national population and served as advocates for their local constituency back home. But, when acting as a single, national body, the members collectively claimed they were then representing the entire population, the entire nation, and that their authority to do so was derived from the people as a whole. The sovereignty of the people, it was declared, rested with the whole of the people of the country, and that sovereign authority was automatically transferred to the whole elected body, the parliament.

Morgan, speaking of the new fiction, writes: "The people to whom they [the parliament] attributed supreme power were themselves fictional and could most usefully remain so, a mystical body, existing as a people only in the actions of the Parliament that claimed to act for them. It would perhaps not be too much to say that representatives invented the sovereignty of the people in order to claim it for themselves...The sovereignty of the people was an instrument by which representatives raised themselves to the maximum distance above the particular set of people who chose them. " (Morgan 1988, 49-50)

While the basic idea of popular sovereignty was eventually exported to America, according to Morgan, three crucial supporting fictions—the invincible yeoman farmer, elections and election campaigns, and a means for the people to instruct their representatives—were needed to make the myth work, to make it more believable in the New World. After all, it is not easy to imagine that this single sovereign body, the whole people, actually exists apart from government, is superior to government and is capable of somehow carrying out major political acts such as creating and abolishing governments. In America, the sovereign people myth needed a cast of supporting lessor myths.

THE INVINCIBLE YEOMAN

The popular sovereign fiction worked well in England, where the common man traditionally deferred political judgments to members of an upper class. But even in the less class-conscious America—where a small elite nonetheless also dominated the political process during the late 1700s—something was needed to assure "the people" that they, in fact, exercised control over their government.

One fictional vehicle for doing so, says Morgan, was "the notion that the ability of the people to exercise sovereignty and control their government rested on the righteousness, independence, and military might of the yeoman farmer, the man who owned his own land, made his living from it, and stood ready to defend it and his country by force of arms." (Morgan 1988, 153-154)

These small landowners looked up to the owners of larger estates as their social superiors and, in this way, helped sell the notion that even in America the many were willing to be governed by the few. The yeomen farmers appeared to be in control when, in fact, they were not.

Today, says Morgan, "We assume too easily that popular sovereignty was the product of popular demand, a rising of the many against the few. It was not. It was a question of some of the few enlisting the many against the rest of the few. Yeomen did not declare their own independence. Their lordly neighbors declared it, in an appeal for support against those other few whom they feared and distrusted as enemies of liberty and to the security of property…[and]…against that unsafe portion of the many whom they [the well-off few] feared and distrusted: paupers and laborers who held no land." (Morgan 1988, 169) In short, by glorifying the yeomen farmers, elite rulers exercised control over them and, at the same time, encouraged the yeomen farmers to more readily submit to their rule.

In the early 1800s, the yeoman farmer myth paved the way for another American myth, the belief in populism—the idea that the political instincts of the common man can be trusted, and even preferred, over those of an elite group. Today the populism myth continues to shore up our view of self-rule by assuring the masses that, through popular protest movements and other grassroots acts, they are still key players in the political arena.

ELECTIONS AND ELECTIONEERING

Elections—public events capable of bringing together and politically elevating persons of all social ranks—represent a critical American institution. From the beginning, Morgan writes, "An election was a time when ordinary men found themselves the center of attention. The frantic solicitation of their votes elevates them to a position of importance they could not dream of at other times….To win votes a man had to prostrate himself before voters, take off his hat to people whom he would not recognize when the election is over….An election too was a safety valve, an interlude when the humble could feel a power otherwise denied them, a power that was only half illusionary. And it was a legitimizing ritual, a rite by which the populace renewed their consent to an oligarchical power structure….Is it too much to say that the choice the voters made was not so much a choice of candidates as it was a choice to participate in the charade and act out the fiction of their own power, renewing their submission by accepting the ritual homage of those who sought their votes?" (Morgan 1988, 195, 206-207)

THE PEOPLE'S VOICE

If the fiction of popular sovereignty is made more acceptable with frequent elections, it is an easy next step for the people to believe they exercise control over their elected representatives with letters, phone calls, demonstrations and other non-binding forms of instruction. While this range of communications may make the masses feel more a part of the governmental process, they remain non-binding for practical reasons. What should an elected representative do if contradictory instructions are voiced by his or her constituents? In addition, what if a minority group, with the financial resources to communicate louder than other groups, could, through their elected representative, bind the entire district's population to their own narrow interests.

Today the Internet has pumped new life into this old myth. Virtually all elected officials have set up websites and e-mailboxes to receive instructions from voters. And the ease with which voters can now electronically advise their representatives has multiplied the traffic flow from citizen to representative many fold. It remains to be seen, however, if this electronic pipeline between the people and their representatives actually gives the people greater control over the behavior of their elected representatives. Perhaps the Internet is actually performing the role of a political placebo and making it easier for the many to submit to rule by the few.

* * * * *

When all is said and done, the American democracy is, in large part, make believe. The few necessarily rule the many but, since the few must gain the consent of the masses to rule effectively, they must constantly work to make sure political reality does not stray too far from political fictions.

What happens when young citizens become aware that the real American democracy that they live in does not work as described in the schoolbooks? What they do is nothing less than the pivotal act of good citizens. For sure, some feel cheated and drop out, becoming permanently alienated from public life. But for the vast majority of the citizens, as long as the real-life democracy remains not too far removed from their cherished democratic myths, they will simply play along and pretend to believe in what they know to be untrue—to suspend their disbelief in political myths to make democracy work.

"The success of government," says Morgan, "thus requires the acceptance of fictions, requires the willing suspension of disbelief, requires us to believe that the emperor is clothed even though we can see that he is not...Government requires make-believe... Make believe that the people have a voice or make believe that the representatives of the people are the people. Make believe that all men are equal or make believe that they are not…a fiction must bear some resemblance to fact. If it strays too far from fact the willing suspension of disbelief collapses…I do not imply deception or delusion on the part of those who employed or subscribed to the fictions described here, fictions in which they willingly suspended disbelief. My purpose is not to debunk, but to explore the wonder that Hume points to, the fact that most of us submit willingly to be governed by the few of us." (Morgan 1988, 13-15)

How Citizens Suspend Their Disbelief in Democracy

Theater-goers readily set aside reality and enter a make-believe world unfolding onstage before them. To work, stage productions containing magic spells, mythical creatures and heroes flying through the air call upon their viewers to accept these fictions as real. In other words, to enjoy the show, the audience must be willing to suspend their disbelief in magic spells, mythical creatures and airborne people.

In politics, too, make believe plays a central, but less visible, role. In fact, as Morgan concludes, American democracy, like a theater production, could not function if its citizens did not believe in certain political fictions. From the nation's very start, political fictions were written into the Declaration of Independence by Thomas Jefferson, including "self-evident" truths and the assertion that a legitimate government must derive its authority from the consent of the governed people. Because these declared beliefs—like all myths—are hard, if not impossible, to prove factually, Morgan dubs them fictions.

Morgan is not trying to discredit the role fictional beliefs play in the political arena. He simply demonstrates how fictions help the governing few retain the allegiance of the many and how myths make it easier for self-governing citizens to submit to rule by others.

Political fictions must be presented in such a way that they invite and allow the many citizens to willingly submit to the will of the few. To maintain control over the many, politicians must make sure reality does not stretch a fiction too far. First, political fictions must be carefully crafted. Then, political institutions—frequent elections, for instance—must be created to maintain those fictions and encourage generations of citizens to willingly accept the fictions as real. Citizens will willingly suspend their disbelief in a political fiction, and thereby accept it as real, only if it does not depart too far from reality. A fiction that is too unlike reality is too unbelievable to be suspended. Table 5 summarizes how citizens use myths to make sense of political reality.

The popular sovereignty fiction works, in large part, because it is presented to school kids as a non-debatable truth. As these students leave school and become adult citizens, the governing few make sure citizens periodically receive the evidence needed to reinforce their belief that they are, in fact, the supreme authority, even as their firsthand political experiences discredit the fiction. Frequent elections, town hall meetings where citizens can directly address elected officials and the use of citizen advisory panels are a few of the many ways in which the popular sovereignty fiction is kept alive and believable.

America's media is also doing its part to keep democratic myths alive. Theodore Lowi and Benjamin Ginsberg contend that, "Americans continue to see every presidential election as an opportunity to reset the nation's course and correct the mistakes of the past. The public is generally content to listen to the promises of change and new beginnings during the new administration's honeymoon period, while even the most jaded journalists usually suspend disbelief and write paeans to the new administration's dazzling personalities, policies and ideas." (Lowi & Ginsberg 1995, 3)

TABLE 5

How Citizens Use Myths

A democratic myth is accepted as true.
But then political reality does not conform to the myth.
Faith in the myth shifts from acceptance to doubt.
What to do?
a.) Citizens can accept political reality and abandon their existing faith in the myth, or
b.) They can accommodate political reality by willingly suspending their disbelief in the myth and pretending the myth remains true.

How Citizens Depend on Myths

While Morgan focused on how political myths allow citizens in a self-rule democracy to willingly submit to rule by the few, Murray Edelman, in *The Symbolic Uses of Politics*, takes a closer look at how political rites and myths are used by citizens to interpret and attach meaning to personally experienced political acts and, in the process, to buy into the sovereign people myth.

POLITICAL RITES are public actions and activities that, by bringing citizens together, create a patriotic bond within a population. Examples are all around us. Town meetings frequently start with a pledge of allegiance to the American flag. Sporting events often start with the national anthem. In 2011, for example, more than 73 million persons attended major league baseball games and stood at attention while the national anthem was sung. Professional football games attracted more than 17 million fans, basketball 21 million and ice hockey another 20 million—and in each case, fans enthusiastically express a collective feeling of nationhood as they stand to sing, or listen to, the national anthem. Add to these numbers college and high school sporting event attendees and television viewers at home, and the reach of this one national, patriotic ritual is overwhelming.

By participating in political events, as active participants or spectators, citizens adopt and reinforce existing political norms. In addition, political rites are used by citizens to overcome doubts about their role in the political system. If news reports create uncertainty as to whether self-rule really exists in America, political debates, actions of state and federal legislatures—and especially election campaigns and the act of casting ballots—all reinforce a popular impression that the political system does, in fact, listen to citizens and acts to turn their desires into public policies.

POLITICAL MYTHS, as defined by Edelman, signify "a belief held in common by a large group of people that gives events and actions a particular meaning." (Edelman 1971, 14) While political rites involve the active participation of citizens in political events, political myths create belief systems that are widely accepted by citizens as valid, without question, including belief in "the rational character of the voting act, the reality of the

controls elections exert over government policy directions..."
(Edelman 1985, 18)

Edelman adds an example of how myths work: "Americans are taught at home, in the schools and in pervasive political rhetoric that America is the land of opportunity; that there is equality before the law; that government accurately reflects the voice of the people, but does not shape it; that political and economic values are allocated fairly. Given such opportunity, those who are poor are inclined to attribute their unhappy condition to their own failings and inadequacies...In consequence the poor have typically been meek, acquiescent in their role and status, and grateful for the welfare benefits they receive: benefits whose very meagerness further defines the worth of the recipients." (Edelman 1971, 55)

Edelman goes on to say, "Without them [rites and myths] the inequities in wealth, in income, and in influence over governmental allocations of resources can be expected to bring restiveness; with them potential rebellion is displaced by 'constitutional' criticism or approval." (Edelman 1985, 18)

Since political myths are held by citizens prior to witnessing political events or the actions of government officials, myths are used to interpret the significance of public events or actions. And, by knowing beforehand the myths citizens hold about democracy, a government official can anticipate—and manipulate—how political events or actions will be received by spectators. For example, during economic hard times, politicians dead set against extending unemployment payments might tap into the American self-made-man myth to rally unemployed workers to exercise more personal responsibility and to try harder to land a job.

Importantly, rites and myths are not mandated by the political system nor are they necessarily invented by elite groups to deceive and exploit the masses. The masses themselves eagerly adopt myths to make sense of and define their political roles and to guide their behavior as individual citizens. Elite groups simply seize the opportunities popular political myths open up for them.

Political rites and myths place beyond question the fundamental ideas and values upon which the American democracy rests—including the very idea of popular government and that citizens are in control of their government. By clinging to the myth that their government serves the public interest, citizens tend to drop their guard, become distracted and open the door for political shenanigans by well-organized interest groups seeking government favors and benefits largely out of sight of a politically passive, We the People.

While participation in political rituals—especially election spectacles—and belief in political myths afford individual

TABLE 6

How Governments Actually Work

Beliefs About How Governments Work	How Governments Actually Work
We tell ourselves that we the people determine what government will do, and we point to elections, legislative actions, and 'soundings' of the public as evidence.	What people get from government is what administrators do about their problems rather than the promises of statutes, constitutions, or oratory.
We believe that our machinery of government functions so that administrators carry out the will of the legislature and, therefore, of the people, rather than making policy by themselves.	The assumption by the mass public that what administrators do is ordained by a legislative and public 'will' sanctifies administrative actions and helps make them acceptable.
We tell ourselves that government has the power and knowledge to produce the results the people want [and] we assure ourselves that a government that satisfies public demands thereby wins popular support…This belief is basic to our faith in popular sovereignty.	It can rarely be known what concrete future effects public laws and acts will bring [but the people] want to believe that officials have the power and knowledge to produce particular results.

Source: Edelman 1985, 192-194.

citizens fleeting and largely symbolic satisfaction with the performance of the American democratic system, between elections these same myths tend to pacify citizens and provide a green light for elite groups to exercise real, lasting influence over government actions and public policies and win tangible, not symbolic, benefits.

Here, in Table 6, is how Edelman contrasts popular beliefs held by citizens as to how American governments should work with how governments actually work.

Myths in Action

My guess is that a majority of American citizens believe that at least some of the myths described in this book are true or, if not, they conveniently suspend their disbelief and pretend the myths are true. But these myths are far more than just stories. In the real world of American politics, the power of myths is hugely magnified, and some even gain the status of unquestioned dogma.

Democratic myths are so deeply implanted in Americans in schools, and then reinforced in rituals and rites and symbols and songs, that to flatly deny their truth is almost unthinkable—not unlike the reluctance of doubting Christians to question the existence of God. If for most Americans flat denial of democratic myths is out of the question, suspension of disbelief is a widely accepted way to personally, and privately, deny their truth and, at the same time, to publicly appear to confirm their truth.

In the hands of politicians, lawmakers, advocacy groups, self-serving interest groups—and even the Supreme Court—myths provide the essential political grease needed to push public issues one way or the other. By framing public issues in a manner that taps into widely held myths, politicians are able to gain the needed support, or at least the passive acquiescence, of the citizens.

Table 7 lists some of the ways in which American democratic myths and current political issues can be tied one to the other in day-to-day politics.

TABLE 7

Myths Linked to Government Policies

Citizens who accept these democratic myths may...	...Support government policies that
Individualism – the belief that good citizens depend on self-reliance, not help from the government.	1.) Oppose government provided health care. 2.) Lower taxes & provide fewer government services. 3.) Privatize public services. 4.) With NRA, oppose gun control laws. 5.) Equate what is good for the individual is good for society. 6.) Deregulate mining, banking & finance industries.
Antistatism - the belief that strong central governments put personal liberties at risk.	1.) Cut taxes; starve the government beast. 2.) Define big government as Un-American. 3.) Call for less intrusion into the daily lives of citizens. 4.) Support the Tea Party.
Popular Sovereignty – the belief that the people are the ultimate political power in an elected, representative democracy, and governments are subject to the will of the people.	1.) Give Americans greater control over their government. 2.) Give citizens greater access to elections as a dependable means for the people to exercise their political power. Even the U.S. Supreme Court supports this myth. To justify its 2010 ruling in Citizens United v. Federal Election Commission that, "political speech must prevail against laws that would suppress it," the court's five person majority cited a 1976 Supreme Court case: "In a republic where the people are sovereign, the ability of the citizenry to make informed choices among candidates for office is essential." And to support its claim that corporate campaign contributions do not corrupt the election process, the court cited a 1957 Supreme Court case: "Under our Constitution it is We The People who are sovereign. The people have the final say. The legislators are their spokesmen..."

Populism – the belief that citizens possess the free will and wisdom to manage their own political fate.	1.) Increase citizen participation in government decision-making processes. 2.) Reject rule by elite groups. 3.) Support Occupy Wall Street demonstrations. 4.) Save the family farm (a modern day version of 18th century faith that democracy depended on the yeoman farmer). 5.) Use scientific polls and Internet-based social media to muster grassroots support for or against government policies and actions. 6.) Call for greater citizen-made laws and political control using initiative, referendum and recall powers.
Self-rule – the belief that, in America, the people rule themselves through a representative democracy.	1.) Encourage political party tactics to get out and vote. 2.) Promote elections as a trusted and effective tool for the people to exercise their political power. The U.S. Supreme Court's majority opinion in Citizens United v. Federal Election Commission cited the self-rule myth when it wrote, "The right of citizens to inquire, to hear, to speak, and to use information to reach consensus is a precondition to enlightened self-government and a necessary means to protect it."
Egalitarianism – the belief that in economic and political affairs, all citizens are guaranteed an equal opportunity – but not necessarily equal results.	1.) Justify economic inequality as inevitable. 2.) Suggest anyone can become president, or a millionaire. 3.) Support gender, racial or economic based groups demanding equal rights.

CHAPTER FIVE

What Is Your Citizenship Style?

"Constitutional democracy is based upon the political responsibility of the individual citizen, because it rests upon the consent of most of the governed."

(Spiro 1969, 28)

* * * * *

Make believe is no substitute for the real thing. We are now, as a nation, but also as individual citizens, at a crossroad, a place where we need to individually take stock of how well our political myths and our political reality fit together into a workable, acceptable whole. Is the American experiment with democracy, set in motion long years ago, simply too difficult for the average American to put into practice today? The preceding chapters have, I hope, prepared you to take the next step, to sort out where you fit, as a citizen, in our two-part (part real, part make believe) democracy.

Keep in mind as you work through this chapter how the two divergent parts of American democracy play out. **Political myths** describe a governing system in which citizens play a central, powerful role. On the other hand, **political reality** describes a governing system dominated by wealthy campaign contributors, interest groups and their lobbyists.

* * * * *

Are you: a Self-rule Idealist; a Self-rule Pragmatist; a Civic Fatalist or a Civic Dropout? Let's find out!

Start with Table 8
Down the table's left side, choose the description that best fits your view concerning political myths: Do you, on balance, accept democracy as described by political myths, or do you see these myths as weak or non-existent? If you strongly accept what the myths stand for, you may classify yourself as either a Self-rule Idealist or a Self-rule Pragmatist. If you do not view our government as defined by the myths described earlier, you may classify yourself as a Civic Fatalist or a Civic Dropout.

Next, reading across the top of Table 8, do you see a wide gap separating the democracy described by the political myths described earlier and the real democracy you know based on your personal experiences, or do you consider the gap to be small or non-existent? If you see a wide gap between the self-rule myths and the way American democracy really operates, you may classify yourself as a Self-rule Idealist or a Civic Fatalist. If you do not see a wide myth-reality gap, you might be more accurately described as a Self-rule Pragmatist or a Civic Dropout.

Once you have located yourself on the left side of the table and across the top, where your two selected preferences intersect defines your current citizenship style. For example, if you have a strong belief in the democracy described by myths and see a large gap separating the mythical ideals and political reality, you appear to be a Self-rule Idealist. If, on the other hand, you do not strongly believe in the myths and you see little or no myth vs. reality gap, you are likely a Civic Dropout.

Table 9
To further test whether the citizenship style you assigned to yourself in Table 8 is right for you, go to Table 9, where you will find a list of characteristics associated with each citizenship style. Do you identify with some or all of the characteristics listed in Table 9 for the citizenship style you assigned to yourself in Table 8? If you do, your chosen citizenship style is confirmed. If not, go back and recalculate where you place yourself on Table 8.

Table 10
Table 10 is an attempt to project, over time, the evolution of citizens from high school to their adoption of a final, experience-based, citizenship lifestyle. I admit that Table 10, in the absence of actual data, is simply an educated guess, but I believe the table is accurate enough for our purposes. That is, it is safe to say that most citizens do change their citizenship style over time as they leave school behind and gain firsthand experience. The guesswork comes in where I assign hypothetical percentages for the share of the adult population occupying each citizenship style category. Still, I contend the assigned percentages are good enough to demonstrate how your personal citizenship style might shift over time.

Why do You Feel Politically Powerless?
Let's go back to Chapter Three for a moment. Three possible causes of your powerlessness feelings were examined: citizens themselves failing to act as citizens, a political system that pushes citizens to the sidelines, and a political system captured by a few ruling elite groups or individuals. With which of these possible causes did you most identify?

If you found citizens or elites to be the most likely culprits, you may already possess the citizen characteristics associated with a Self-rule Idealist—or you may want to seriously consider becoming one. Why? Because of the four citizenship lifestyles found in Table 8, Self-rule Idealists are very much in the business of strengthening the role of citizens in the governmental process. In addition, greater citizen engagement is one way to lessen the political grip of elites.

If, on the other hand, you favor the case for a rigged political system, you might conclude that elected term limits, public financing of elections and other system management fixes are the answer rather than the promotion of more engaged citizens.

If You Are a Self-rule Pragmatist

So, you have labeled yourself—along with many millions of your fellow citizens—a Self-rule Pragmatist, a citizen eager to believe, or pretend, that the democratic myths are really true. This is where, I contend, most high school graduates start their civic lives as adults. Even as evidence piles up to show the myths are probably not true, you hang on to your belief in the myths, you continue to believe they truly define the operation of the American democracy. *This denial of reality is the root cause of your feeling of political powerlessness.*

An important difference exists between the behavior of Self-rule Pragmatists and Self-rule Idealists. Pragmatists are content to accept democratic myths as true and accept them as a reasonably accurate description of reality. Idealists know the myths do not reflect reality and, through active civic participation, work to make the myths come true—to make reality conform to the myths.

The big problem is simply this: America has far too few Self-rule Idealists and way too many Self-rule Pragmatists. The only way the American democracy will right itself is for a mass migration of citizens from the pragmatist camp to the idealist camp.

As a Self-rule Pragmatist, you reluctantly acknowledge evidence that maybe the democratic myths are not a true description of our democracy. You are, of course, free to accept these myths and to remain blissfully content with your current citizenship role.

Your options: stay put, continue to ignore your growing disbelief in the democratic myths. As you struggle to mentally close the myth-reality gap, you can continue to tell pollsters how, as a citizen, you feel powerless and politically marginalized.

Or, you might think about moving into the Self-rule Idealist arena, filled with citizens willing to rock the boat. You can keep your belief in the democratic myths intact, as before; however, as a Self-rule Idealist, you will no longer need to suspend your disbelief in the myths and deny the gap's existence. No sir! As a Self-rule Idealist, your new mission will be to expose the gap, to focus on ways to bring political reality in line with the democratic myths. You will trade in life in a fictional democracy for an active role in the real American democracy.

Once the democratic myths are exposed for what they are, good citizens get busy pushing democratic reality toward the myth-based democracy being taught to our school kids, including:

- running for office;
- signing petitions seeking government action;
- writing letters to public officials voicing your position on public issues;
- writing letters to newspapers voicing one's position on a public issue;
- supporting a candidate's election campaign by contributing money or working on his or her campaign staff;
- performing volunteer work in a community organization;
- attending political rallies;
- making a public speech;
- writing an article for publication on a political topic, or
- joining a reform group.

Your only other options are long shots, since they will require that you renounce your long-held belief in the sacred democratic myths. Becoming a Civic Fatalist or a Civic Dropout is out of the question so long as you are a believer. If, however, you see the gap separating the myths and political reality growing larger and larger, you may feel less and less comfortable as a Self-rule Pragmatist. When you can no longer, with a clear conscience, pretend the myths are real, you might want to take another look at becoming a Civic Fatalist or a Civic Dropout.

As the political landscape in America becomes more and more polarized, more dog eat dog and the myths that enhance the political power of citizens become more and more beyond belief, you might want to shed your Self-rule Pragmatist cape and retreat into democracy's backwoods of the Civic Fatalists and the Civic Dropouts. Until that day arrives, however, your only options are to buck up and become an active Self-rule Idealist, or stay put as a Self-rule Pragmatist.

If you are a Self-rule Idealist

The life of a Self-rule Idealist is not an easy one. You are up against an entrenched foe, powerful interest groups that know how to take advantage of myth-believing citizens and coopt government agencies for their own selfish benefit. You may need to accept disappointment as a way of life, with only an occasional victory to boost your spirits and keep you going. But, you can hold your head high, for you and your fellow Self-rule Idealists are putting into practice the "civic virtues" the nation's founders believed to be an essential ingredient in a democracy. A few good citizens may be all the American democracy needs to stay afloat. But what happens when you burn out, when you are too tired to continue the good fight? Where do you go then? As long as your belief in the democratic myths remains strong, you might think about becoming a Self-rule Pragmatist. The hardest part, after years of fighting to close the huge gap between myths and reality, will be to shift gears and accept that the myth-reality gap is either small or non-existent. If you can't do that, you will not be a happy Self-rule Pragmatist.

Would you fit as Civic Fatalist or a Civic Dropout? Probably not. For one thing, you are a citizen of action. Civic Fatalists and Civic Dropouts are not. In addition, you find it hard to turn your back on your belief that civic participation is a civic duty; Civic Fatalists and Civic Dropouts are experts at doing so.

The bottom line: Self-rule Idealists are trapped. Your civic role is not easily traded in for another. Your best course of action is steady as she goes, always looking for new ways to take ground from the special interests and return the political territory to its rightful owner—the American people.

If you are a Civic Fatalist

If you classify yourself as a Civic Fatalist, you probably moved to this citizenship style from elsewhere. Your earlier style may have been that of a Self-rule Idealist or Pragmatist. As a prior Self-rule Idealist, you may have quit working to close the myth-reality gap and empower the people—in line with the cherished democratic myths—due to civic exhaustion or a feeling of utter futility. Perhaps you abandoned an earlier Self-rule Pragmatist style because you could no longer pretend the democratic myths were, in fact, the driving force in the American system of government.

But what can you do now? Have you considered charging your civic batteries and joining or re-joining the Self-rule Idealists? What is holding you back? Civic inertness? Fear of failure?

If you are a Civic Dropout

I hope I have not unfairly treated you and all other citizens who place themselves in this do-nothing category. There are, I suspect, many sound reasons for a person to escape from his or her citizenship responsibilities. My only point here is that in a self-rule democracy, every citizen has an obligation to do his or her part—large or small—to make it work. In a healthy democracy, dropping out should not be an option.

TABLE 8

What Is Your Citizenship Style?

	You see a WIDE GAP separating political myths and political reality	You see a SMALL or NO GAP separating political myths and political reality
YOU ACCEPT the principles promoted in American political myths	**Self-rule Idealist** You Assume: The people are the supreme political power. You tend to highlight the gap, find it unacceptable and, by moving political reality toward the democratic myths, hope to narrow the gap. Motto: Power to the people.	**Self-rule Pragmatist** You Assume: The people are relatively powerless, but that's OK. You tend to hide the gap by denying its existence or reluctantly accepting it as the way to rationalize and balance democratic ideals and political facts of life. Motto: What you see is what you get.
YOU DO NOT ACCEPT the principles promoted in American political myths	**Civic Fatalist** You Assume: The myth vs. reality gap is inevitable. The few will always rule the many. Motto: You can't fight city hall.	**Civic Dropout** You Assume: Political alienation, where citizens have little or nothing to do with government, makes a lot of sense. Motto: Democracy is rigged against the little guy.

TABLE 9

Citizenship Style Descriptors

Self-rule Idealists...

- Assume governments are formed "Of, by, and for the people."
- Favor more "direct democracy" (initiatives, referendum and recalls) to replace or augment indirect, elected representative democracy.
- Are active in organizations promoting greater citizen participation— the League of Women Voters and local school boards, for example.
- Work as volunteers on behalf of candidates in election campaigns.
- Are found along the entire public issues spectrum: anti-tax libertarians, Occupy Wall Street demonstrators, Mothers Against Drunk Driving, members of the religious right and some favor and some oppose President Obama's healthcare reforms.
- Stay well-informed by reading newspapers or watching TV news broadcasts.

Self-rule Pragmatists...

- Limit their political activity to occasionally voting in elections.
- Believe politicians listen to special interest lobbyists more than they listen to the people who put them in office: the voters.
- Allow family and job-related matters to take priority over civic duties.
- Are often politically silent, but active as soccer moms, members of community, good works organizations, environmental groups, etc.

Civic Fatalists...

- Consider self-rule democracy an unattainable, pie-in-the-sky dream.
- Are often fallen away Idealists and Self-rule Pragmatists who have lost their faith in myth-based democracy.
- Explain away the political reality in America as a rigged sham favoring the political elite.
- Accept most elected officials as self-serving opportunists.
- Can be found complaining about politics at the local American Legion bar.

Civic Dropouts...

- Unlike Civic Fatalists who once believed in the democratic myths. Civic dropouts never personally accepted their citizenship responsibilities. They have, from the start, viewed themselves outside of the governmental process.
- Join back-to-the-land or off-the-grid self-sufficiency groups.
- Might be called anarchists or support "starve the beast," anti-tax, anti-government policies.

TABLE 10

Three-Part Citizenship Life Cycle

Starting Point			
American high schools send citizens-to-be into civic life armed with myth-based, schoolbook democracy.			
Mid-Course Correction Stage			
Self-rule Idealist	**Self-rule Pragmatist**	**Civic Fatalist**	**Civic Dropout**
From school, a small number, perhaps 5%, of young adult citizens start here. * * * ADD 10% of Self-rule Pragmatists wanting to become more active and work to empower citizens. SUBTRACT 5% of burned out Self-rule Idealists who join Civic Fatalists or Self-rule Pragmatists.	From school, a majority, up to 85% of young adult citizens, start out here. * * * SUBTRACT 10% who move to the Self-rule Idealists camp. SUBTRACT 30% who can no longer pretend the people are politically powerful, and eventually join the Civic Fatalists. ADD up to 5% from Self-rule Idealist camp.	Lacking firsthand experience, few, if any, young adult citizens start here upon leaving school. * * * Only after gaining first-hand experience do disillusioned and burned out citizens reluctantly accept the role of Civic Fatalist. ADD up to 5% from Self-rule Idealist camp. ADD 30% from Self-rule Pragmatist camp.	From school, perhaps as many as 10% of the young adult citizens never develop an appetite for citizenship.
Final, Adopted Citizenship Style			
The final and more or less permanent citizenship style for about 10% of American citizens.	The final and more or less permanent final citizenship style for about 50% of American citizens.	The final and more or less permanent final citizenship style for about 30% of American citizens.	The final and more or less permanent final citizenship style for about 10% of American citizens.

CHAPTER SIX

Where To From Here?

"Cheshire Puss," she began rather timidly..."Would you tell me, please, which way to go from here?"

"That depends a good deal on where you want to get to," said the Cat.

"I don't much care where..." said Alice.

"Then it doesn't matter which way you go," said the Cat."

(*Alice's Adventures in Wonderland*, by Lewis Carroll)

* * * * *

By now you should have a better understanding of both your current citizenship style and why you feel politically powerless.

The citizen participation gap is not a result of lazy or disinterested citizens. The gap is mainly the result of a widespread belief in unfulfilled historical and political myths that has lulled millions of citizens into a false sense of political power and the adoption of an inactive citizenship participation style. Self-serving special interest groups, their lobbyists and wealthy election campaign financiers have rushed into the political vacuum created by the citizen participation gap and rigged the American political system for their own benefit.

Governments in America, as we learn in school, are formed and operated with the consent of the governed citizens. No more. Once in office, elected officials devote themselves to the care and feeding of favor-seeking interest groups and their financial backers, not the people who voted them into office.

How can citizens regain control of their elected officials? The list of past attempts to reform the political system, to decrease the role of money and interest group dominance, is long. Campaign financing reform, public financing of elections, term limits, etc., have all had their day. All have failed to significantly alter the status quo. Why? Because too many elected lawmakers owe their job security to the status quo.

Legal fixes to control special interests are not the answer. The U.S. Supreme Court recently ruled that money is a form of speech, that wealthy corporations have an unlimited right to be "heard." The current legal and legislative systems will continue to favor the powerful interest groups that now dominate the political system until determined, politically active citizens push back and impose change.

It really doesn't matter if citizen participation is going up or down. Either way, current participation levels are inadequate to get the job done. The essential truth is that ONLY with a huge increase in the number of determined and effective citizens working for change, will elected officials remain responsive to the people who put them into office.

If "We the People" formed the political system we now live in, it follows that we are ultimately responsible to make it work. What can be done to level the political playing field, to get the American people back into their self-rule game? And from where will the needed enthusiasm for such change come?

The problem is simply that there are too few Self-rule Idealists to rescue our democracy. What is needed is an awakening of a critical mass of Self-rule Pragmatists committed to closing the myth-reality gap. Until that day arrives, American democracy will remain the plaything of the wealthy, the powerful interest groups and their professional lobbyists.

And what might that critical mass look like? If at least 10% of the Self-rule Pragmatists were to quit believing in democratic myths and begin working to make these myths a reality, as the Self-rule Idealists are currently doing, a new political landscape would begin to emerge with citizens in the driver's seat. In towns and cities across America, thousands of converts will be needed.

There are two possible ways this political realignment can happen.

Education Reform

The long range, slow road to reform is simply to stop setting kids up for failure as adult citizens. Myth-filled schoolbooks now provide a false picture of the actual political power possessed by citizens. At the same time, schools fail to give students the skills needed to perform their assigned civic duties. These twin failures drive citizens out of, not into, the civic arena.

Schools must stop telling our kids they are the supreme political power when, in fact, they are not. At least with the Santa Claus myth, parents have the good sense to tell their kids, sooner or later, that Santa is just that, a myth. We, as a society, do not exercise the same degree of moral responsibility with schoolbook myths. We force each young citizen to find the truth the hard way. And on their road to reality, we alienate citizens and push them out of, not into, the political arena. Kids should leave school with a down-to-earth, realistic picture of the political landscape waiting for them, not fantasy-filled myths that quickly burst when they collide with the real world.

Since the late 1800s, very few politicians have dared refer to the sovereign people, or use the term, "popular sovereignty." Once a popular reference in political speeches, it is now almost exclusively reserved for use in civic textbooks and to indoctrinate school kids. Could it be that the gap separating the sovereign people myth and political reality has grown so wide that the term popular sovereignty is no longer politically credible on Main Street?

The wellbeing of adult citizens is directly dependent on the civic preparation kids receive in school. Poor civic preparation equals poor civic performance. Rebuilding a democracy based on active citizenship would ensure that citizens leave high school with the political awareness and analytical and communications skills needed to play their part to make democracy work by holding elected officials accountable to them, not special interests.

Over time, as millions of young adults leave school equipped to fulfill their role of either self-assured Self-rule Idealists or Self-rule Pragmatists with Self-rule Idealist leanings, greater political power will shift back to where it belongs: with the people.

Citizen Actions
Education reform is only part of the solution. Equally important in the near term is the need to convert thousands of Self-rule Pragmatists into Self-rule Idealists. As the number of Self-rule Pragmatists goes down and the number of Self-rule Idealists goes up, the mythical sovereign people will be replaced with a politically powerful people, in fact.

How might this happen? Once millions of Self-rule Pragmatists take a hard look at the gap separating mythical democracy and real democracy and realize their feelings of political powerlessness is rooted in their belief in unfulfilled myths—the ultimate message of this book—they are likely to trade in their current inactive citizenship lifestyle for a more active one.

And let's not forget the millions of Americans now counted as Civic Fatalists and Civic Dropouts who, by choice, have taken a civic vacation. If, by some miracle, this book lands in their laps, more than a few might decide to give active citizenship another chance.

This popular awakening can't be mandated by law. It can't be implemented with a tempting federal tax break. No one can force citizens to develop the skills and mindset needed to carry out their civic responsibilities. But here is the kicker: no democracy can long survive if too few citizens take their civic responsibilities seriously. No democracy can long survive once the people have outsourced their democracy to the wealthy campaign backers, powerful corporations and their lobbyists.

This political shift depends on discontented—no, angry—citizens who, one by one, conclude that the American democracy is worth saving and that it is up to them to become the kind of citizens our modern-day, self-rule democracy depends on:

citizens determined to reclaim the political process.

In the end, each citizen must ask: Do I care enough about democracy in America to do my part to restore political power to its citizens? Or am I OK with a future in which wealthy political campaign investors, self-serving lobbyists and corporate fat cats continue to hijack the governing process?

Common Cause, formed in 1970 to use "hard-hitting pressure on politicians to bring about results desired by citizens," (Gardner 1972, 15) fell short of its original goals. Since 1970 the American political system has slipped even further from the grasp of the people. Perhaps it is time to rebuild Common Cause or launch a new national citizens lobby.

But wait. No organization can hope to reverse the political decay in America until the citizens themselves are personally committed to that mission. The crucial change that must first take place is not located in an organization. Change will take place only at the individual citizen level. That is where the essential role of active citizens in a healthy democracy must be rediscovered and nurtured. Only then can local and national reform organizations tap into the energy supplied by millions of committed individuals.

What will happen once citizens are aware that their belief in unfulfilled democratic myths has lulled them into a false sense of political wellbeing, that their absence from public forums, their failure to hold elected officials accountable and their failure to support the election of worthy candidates, has placed the American democracy on autopilot and has opened the gate for well-funded, self-serving, special interest groups to take control?

Once it is clear that our once top-rated democracy is now more mythical than real, simple discontentedness with the political system will morph into a feeling of civic shame and guilt and the desire to exercise the political power promised in America's myths will kick in. Once a critical mass of citizens realize they are personally responsible for the sorry condition of our democracy, they will, I hope, roll up their sleeves and get busy rebuilding a government that is responsive to its citizens.

And, best of all, creating governments at all levels responsive to their citizens is not an end in itself. These responsive governments will then become the means to enact reforms that are now blocked by lawmakers controlled by the fat cats. Campaign reforms, common sense environmental policies, more equitable distribution of economic wealth—you name it—will then gain access to the political process.

What are we waiting for?

References

Bachrach, Peter. 1967. *The Theory of Democratic Elitism: A Critique*. Boston and Toronto: Little, Brown and Company.

Barbour, Christine and Gerald C. Wright. 2010. *American Government: Citizenship and Power*. St. Paul, Los Angeles and Indianapolis: EMC Publishing in association with CQ Press.

Bennett, Sharareh Frouzesh. 2005. "An Analysis of the Depiction of Democratic Participation in American Civics Textbooks." Paper presented at the German-American Conference on Responsible Citizenship, Education, and the Constitution, at Freiburg, Germany, September 12-16. Center for Civic Education, Calabasas, California.

Bok, Derek. 2001. *The Trouble with Government*. Cambridge, Massachusetts and London: Harvard University Press.

Bovard, James. 2005. *Attention Deficit Democracy*. New York: Palgrave Macmillan.

Bradley, Phillips, ed. 1945. *Democracy in America, by Alexis De Tocqueville*. Volume I, New York: Vintage Books.

Bradley, Phillips, ed. 1945. *Democracy in America, by Alexis De Tocqueville*. Volume II, New York: Vintage Books.

Bryan, William Jennings. 1896. Bryans' Cross of Gold speech delivered July 9, at the Democratic National Convention in Chicago. http://historymatters.gmu.edu/d/5354/ (Accessed, August 10, 2015)

Burns, James MacGregor, J.W. Peltason, Thomas E. Cronin and David B. Magleby. 1998. *Government by the People*. (Seventeenth Edition). Upper Saddle River, New Jersey: Prentice-Hall, Inc.

Calvert, Robert E. 1991. "Political 'Realism' and Progressive Degradation of Citizenship: A Quiet Constitutional Crisis." In *The Constitution of the People: Reflections on Citizens and Civil Society,* edited by Robert E. Calvert, 127-157. Lawrence, Kansas: University Press of Kansas.

Caplan, Bryan. 2007. "The Myth of the Rational Voter: Why Democracies Choose Bad Policies." Washington, D.C.: CATO Institute Paper No. 594, May 29.

Carnegie Corporation. 2003. *The Civic Mission of Schools.* A Report from Carnegie Corporation of New York and CIRCLE: The Center for Information and Research on Civic Learning and Engagement. New York: CIRCLE and Carnegie Corporation of New York.

Carroll, James D., Walter D. Broadnax, Gloria Contreras, Thomas E. Mann, Norman J. Ornstein and Judith Stiehm. 1987. *We the People: A Review of U.S. Government and Civics Textbooks.* Washington DC: People for the American Way.

Carroll, Lewis. *Alice's Adventures in Wonderland.* New York: Avenel Books, a Division of Crown Publishers, Inc.

Cobb, Roger W. and Charles D. Elder. 1972. *Participation in American Politics: The Dynamics of Agenda-Building.* Baltimore and London: The Johns Hopkins University Press.

Crenson, Matthew A. and Benjamin Ginsberg. 2002. *Downsizing Democracy: How America Sidelined its Citizens and Privatized its Public.* Baltimore and London: The Johns Hopkins University Press.

Dahl, Robert A. *Democracy and its Critics.* 1989. New Haven and London: Yale University Press.

Delli Carpini, Michael X. and Scott Keeter. 1996. *What Americans Know About Politics and Why it Matters.* New Haven and London: Yale University Press.

Dionne, E. J. Jr.1991. *Why* Americans *Hate Politics*. New York: A Touchstone Book published by Simon & Schuster.

Edelman, Murray. 1985. *The Symbolic Uses of Politics*. Urbana and Chicago: University of Illinois Press.

———. 1971. *Politics as Symbolic Action: Mass Arousal and Quiescence*. New York, San Francisco and London: Academic Press, Inc.

Edwards, George C. III, Martin P. Wattenberg and Robert L. Lineberry. 2007. *Government in America: People, Politics, and Policy*, S.O.S. Edition. New York: Pearson Longman.

Edwards, Mickey. 2012. *The Parties Versus the People: How to Turn Republicans and Democrats into Americans*. New Haven and London: Yale University Press.

Eliasoph, Nina. 1998. *Avoiding Politics: How Americans Produce Apathy in Everyday Life*. Cambridge, UK: Cambridge University Press.

Franklin D. Roosevelt Library and Museum. "Roosevelt Facts and Figures." http://www.fdrlibrary.marist.edu/facts.html (Accessed September 7, 2015)

Gallup Historic Trends, "Trust in Government." http://www.gallup.com/poll/5392/trust-government.aspx (Accessed, September 11, 2015)

Gardner, John W. 1972. *In Common Cause*. New York: W.W. Norton & Company, Inc.

Gerster, Patrick and Nicholas Cords. 1997. *Myth America*, Vol II. St James, NY: Brandywine Press.

Goldman, Eric F. 1956. *Rendezvous With Destiny: A History of Modern American Reform*. New York: Vintage Books.

Hart, Peter D. 2004. Peter D. Hart Research Associates, Inc. "Memorandum to C-SPAN from Peter D. Hart Research," dated March 12. Based on a nationwide survey on behalf of C-SPAN.

Hart, Peter D. and Robert Teeter. 1999. "America Unplugged: Citizens and Their Government." Based on a nationwide survey on behalf of the Council for Excellence in Government, May 21 and June 1. http://www.excelgov.org/excel/usunplugged.htm (Accessed, July 13, 1999)

Hibbing, John R. and Elizabeth Theiss-Morse. 2002. *Stealth Democracy: America's Beliefs About How Government Should Work*. Cambridge, UK: Cambridge University Press.

Harcourt School Publishers. 2009. *Harcourt Social* Studies, *North Carolina Geography, History, and Culture*. Boston: Houghton Mifflin Harcourt.

Hamilton, Alexander, James Madison and John Jay. 1911. *The Federalist or the New Constitution*. London: J.M. Dent & Sons Ltd.

Hume, David. 1758. *Of the First Principles of Government*. The Constitution Society. http://www.constitution.org/dh/pringovt.htm (Accessed August 10, 2015)

Jefferson, Thomas. 1787. Letter to James Madison, December 20. http://www.let.rug.nl/usa/presidents/thomas-jefferson/letters-of-thomas-jefferson/jefl66.php (Accessed, August 9, 2015)

———. 1810. Letter to John Tyler, May 26. http://www.let.rug.nl/usa/presidents/thomas-jefferson/letters-of-thomas-jefferson/jefl205.php (Accessed, August 9, 2015)

Kohut, Andrew, Carroll Doherty, Michael Dimock and Scott Keeter. 2011. "Beyond Red vs. Blue: Political Typology." Pew Research Center for the People & the Press, May 4.

Lipscomb, Andrew and Albert Ellery Bergh, eds. 2000. *The Writings of Thomas Jefferson,* Vol. 1, Chapter 4, Document 34. Chicago: The University of Chicago Press.

Lowi, Theodore J. 1969. *The End of Liberalism: Ideology, Policy and the Crisis of Public Authority*. New York: W.W. Norton & Company, Inc.

Lowi, Theodore J. and Benjamin Ginsberg. 1995. *Embattled Democracy: Politics and Policy in the Clinton Era*. New York and London: W.W. Norton & Company.

Martin, Roscoe C. 1957. *Grass Roots*. New York: Harper Colophon Books.

Lundberg, Ferdinand. 1989. *The Myth of Democracy*. New York: Carol Publishing Group.

McClenaghan, William A. 2003. *Magruder's American Government*. Needham, Massachusetts and Upper Saddle, New Jersey: Pearson Prentice Hall.

Morgan, Edmund, S.1988. *Inventing the People: The Rise of Popular Sovereignty in England and America*. New York & London: W.W. Norton & Company.

Morone, James A. 1990. *The Democratic Wish: Popular Participation and the Limits of American Government*, (Revised Edition). New Haven and London: Yale University Press.

Morrow, William L. 1980. *Public Administration: Politics, Policy, and the Political System*. New York: Random House.

Pew Research Center, "U.S. Politics & Policy." November 13, 2014. http://www.people-press.org/2014/11/13/public-trust-in-government/ (Accessed, September 11, 2015)

Pranger, Robert J. 1968. *The Eclipse of Citizenship: Power and Participation in Contemporary Politics*. New York: Holt, Rinehart and Winston, Inc.

Quigley, Charles N. 2007. *National Study Reveals Civics Deficit in U.S. Schools*. Press release, Center for Civic Education. Calabasas, CA., May 16.

Robertson, James Oliver. 1980. *American Myth, American Reality*. New York: Hill & Wang.

Roelofs, H. Mark and Gerald L. Houseman. 1983. *The American Political System: Ideology and Myth*. New York: Macmillan Publishing Co., Inc.

Rosenthal, Alan. 1988. *The Decline of Representative Democracy: Process, Participation, and Power in State Legislatures*. Washington, D.C.: CQ Press.

Saffell, David C. 1998. *Civics: Responsibilities and Citizenship*. New York: Glencoe McGraw-Hill.

Sandel, Michael J. 1996. *Democracy's Discontent: America in Search of a Public Philosophy*. Cambridge, Massachusetts: The Belknap Press of the Harvard University Press.

Schattschneider, E. E. 1960. *The Semisovereign People: A Realist's View of Democracy in America*. New York: Holt, Rinehart and Winston.

Shafritz, Jay M and Albert C. Hyde. 1978. *Classics in Public Administration*. Oak Park, Illinois: Moore Publishing Company, Inc.

Skocpol, Theda. 2003. *Diminished Democracy: From Membership to Management in American Civic Life*. Norman: University of Oklahoma Press.

Spiro, Herbert J. 1969. *Responsibility in Government: Theory and Practice.* New York: Van Nostrand Reinhold Company.

Task Force on Inequality and American Democracy. 2004. *American Democracy in an Age of Rising Inequality.* American Political Science Association.

University of California at Berkeley, Department of Geography. "The Living New Deal," http://livingnewdeal.org/what-was-the-new-deal/programs/ (Accessed, August 10, 2015)

University of California at Santa Barbara, The American Presidency Project. "Voter Turnout in Presidential Elections: 1828-2012." http://www.presidency.ucsb.edu/data/turnout.php (Accessed, August 10, 2015)

White, Leonard D. 1939. *Introduction to the Study of Public Administration.* Revised Edition. New York: The Macmillan Company.

Wiebe, Robert H. 1995. *Self-Rule: A Cultural History of American Democracy.* Chicago and London: The University of Chicago Press.

Wilson, Woodrow. 1887. "The Study of Administration." *Political Science Quarterly*, Vol. II, No. 1.

Zukin, Cliff, Scott Keeter, Molly Andolina, Krista Jenkins and Michael X. Delli Carpini. 2006. *The New Engagement? Political Participation, Civic Life, and the Changing American Citizen.* New York: Oxford University Press.

www.ingramcontent.com/pod-product-compliance
Lightning Source LLC
Chambersburg PA
CBHW052033270326
41931CB00012B/2478